THE
Busy Moms
GUIDE TO
Novel
Marketing

ANGELA CASTILLO
& JAMIE FOLEY

10 Digit ISBN: 0998207845
13 Digit ISBN: 978-0998207841
AISN: B07BR32PNF

Published in Bastrop, Texas

Printed in the United States of America

Glossary

TO OUR *children.*

YOU ARE ALL STRONG, BRAVE, AND BEAUTIFUL.
WE THANK GOD FOR YOU EVERY DAY.

Chapter 1

MY BOOK IS AMAZING,
SO WHY DO I HAVE TO MARKET IT?

"The best marketing doesn't feel like marketing."

— Tom Fishburne

You've done it. You poured your soul into your writing and created a masterpiece of blood, sweat, and tears. You got an awesome cover and published your novel to fly on to glory.

So why isn't it selling itself?

Unfortunately, the marketplace is extremely saturated for ebooks and paperbacks alike. Amazon Kindle alone offers millions of books for sale, and that number grows daily. So how can you get your book to stand out and earn sales in an ocean of competition? And how can indie (self-published) authors hope to compete with the few chosen darlings of the Big 5 publishers?

If you've read our other books, you know that marketing is near and dear to our hearts. Prepare to have the power of our guerrilla mama bear marketing tactics unleashed on your writing career!

We have used these methods to sell books for years—both ours and our clients'—and they *work*. Of course, the Internet and its inner workings are constantly changing, so strategies must be tweaked on occasion, but the basic principles we will share with you have succeeded for quite some time for hundreds of authors in multiple genres.

This book contains marketing help for every type of author, although indie books tend to have the most freedom and flexibility when it comes to marketing. Some of our strategies also work better for different genres. Nonfiction and children's books tend to perform better with different means, but if you're a career novelist, these tips and tricks are right up your alley.

Are we guaranteeing you a million dollars profit every month? Are we assuring you of X amount of sales in X amount of time? Absolutely not, and we would be irresponsible to promise those things. What we *will* do is give you the tools to give your books the best possible chance of getting noticed—and purchased.

We are assuming that you have a book or a series to sell already. If you don't, you might want to check out our other two books first: *The Busy Mom's Guide to Writing* and *The Busy Mom's Guide to Indie Publishing*. Not saying this book won't have helpful hints for you in the long run, but you won't really be able to use most of the principles here until you are close to publishing your book.

WHY SHOULD I LISTEN TO THESE TWO CRAZY MOMS?

We don't like talking about ourselves, or the appearance of bragging (cringe). But since credentials are kind of important in this situation, here are a few reasons why we hope we're in a good position to help others.

Angela

Angela Castillo has been indie publishing since 2014. She's written or co-written fourteen books and numerous short stories of various genres, but she's best known for her bestselling historical series, *Texas Women of Spirit*. The first book in the series, *The River Girl's Song*, has over 300 reviews on Amazon.com and has sold thousands of copies in its first two years. She's spoken at many events, participated in countless more, and has led a short story project with dozens of writers across the globe which has resulted in bestselling status on Amazon.com for all three books in the series *(Steampunk Fairy Tales)*.

Jamie

Jamie Foley worked as a digital marketing specialist for HarperCollins Publishers' Live Events division for three years. As one of the 'Big 5' publishers, HarperCollins had plenty of books to promote, and Jamie was in charge of several websites, email lists, social media, and digital marketing campaigns. She resigned in 2012 to focus on writing her own fantasy novels, including *The Sentinel Trilogy*, but she didn't stop helping other authors on the side with marketing and indie publishing. Her clients include several bestselling authors including Beth Wiseman, as well as companies like Author Media and Uncommon Universes Press.

I ALREADY WROTE A BOOK. FOR CRYING OUT LOUD, NOW I HAVE TO MARKET IT, TOO?

Well, technically, no. You don't *have* to do anything once you hit the button and upload your file to the Kindle store. But the chances of your novel being noticed among the millions of Amazon books and blossoming into a bestselling product all by itself are limited. Not impossible, but pretty slim. Like, winning the lottery slim.

Think about all those hours and days pounding keys, editing, and trying to come up with the perfect name for your sparkly fuschia unicorn. It would be nice if someone actually *read* the book after all your blood, sweat, and tears, right? And even better if you made back your investment on it—plus some gravy on the side.

But unfortunately, books don't sell themselves. Even the best ones.

Some genres are harder to market than others (check out Chapter 12 for more info). Not every book will be a bestseller, and not every book will thrive under our suggested strategies. But almost every book has an audience waiting, and we will do our best to help you find yours.

We can't tell you how many writers have come up to us and said, "I wrote an amazing book, and it has a gorgeous cover and I did everything I was supposed to. But it's not selling! What did I do wrong?"

The first question we ask is always, "What are you doing to promote your book?"

"Well, I've told my friends and family about it, but I thought if I just put it up on Amazon, everyone would want to buy it."

Cue the crickets.

WRITING AN AWESOME BOOK IS ONLY HALF THE BATTLE

We've been selling books for a long time—on Amazon.com, in local bookstores, and even in countries we'd never heard of (where is Malta, anyway?). In our ventures, we've talked to indie writers all over the world. There are a very few amazing writers who had the right idea at the right time, caught the perfect niche market, and started selling hundreds of books the moment their book launched with almost no publicity.

We included this scenario just to make the point that, okay, it *can* happen. But it's very rare. Like potty-training-your-child-in-one-day rare. So most of us can't count on that. We need a plan. Actually, many plans. Or more of a prism-like multifaceted plan with rainbows gently swirling against a freshly-painted wall … (sorry, Angela went into poet mode. Happens when she starts thinking about math too much).

To get your book written, you probably set aside a certain amount of time each work day to write. Now we suggest that you set aside another portion of time per day or week for marketing. We know it's a sacrifice, but we promise it will be worth it.

How much time, you ask? Different authors will have different preferences and goals, but we suggest at least three hours every week. As you move forward, you'll figure out if you need more or can get by on less. You might do most of your marketing work in one set time a week, or you might spend a few minutes every day on various projects.

Why put time into marketing? Well, if you're like most of us, you put a great deal of time into writing your book. And yes, writing is a great form of self-expression, but chances are you really want to share that book. With as many people as possible. And maybe make some money in the process.

Hey. Your book is worth the effort.

ADVERTISING WORKS

A note

If you have books published by a traditional company, you've realized the hard truth: most authors are expected to market their creations, even if their manuscript was bought by a large publisher.

We hope you can find some helpful methods in this book as well, but please check with your publisher about their policies before you get going. Some companies are particular about their methods, branding, and timing of promotions, and we don't want anyone getting into hot water because of us. A selection of our marketing tips will be more useful for indie authors who have absolute control over pricing and marketing strategies.

But that doesn't mean there aren't plenty of good morsels in here for you, too! More and more traditional authors are indie publishing on the side, and gathering knowledge about how the market works will serve you well in your career.

How many things have you purchased because you saw an advertisement? Maybe a commercial caught your interest, or a viral video, or a magazine ad on Black Friday. Perhaps it was that new Roomba on a fancy endcap display. Or someone was handing out free samples of your favorite chocolate at the Sweet-Tooths-R-Us. Or, let's face it, your kid might have thrown a tantrum because you foolishly went down the wrong aisle in the grocery store (what evil minion hangs toys in the light bulb section?). Millions of dollars are spent every month on advertising in the US because advertising works, pure and simple.

The very real and difficult truth is that some authors never get discovered. Thousands of wonderful books are out there that have never been opened, never read—simply because they were not advertised. They have not been marketed properly to their genre's target audience, and therefore no one knows about them.

Sometimes we need to pay for our work to be featured on a platform—a popular website, blog, podcast, or even radio or TV—to get the word out to our target audience. The three most popular paid promotions for books nowadays are:

1. Large email lists that offer deals to their vast readership, such as BookBub
2. Sponsored ads on social media or sales platforms such as Facebook and Amazon
3. Spotlights on blogs and websites with a specific readership

We aren't telling you to just go throw hundreds of dollars into advertising every month and hope it works. You need a game plan. And that's why we're here.

CAN I MAKE A PROFIT IF I ONLY HAVE ONE BOOK TO SELL?

Yes. Whether your book is a stand-alone or the first in a series, you can make sales on one book, and we definitely think you should do your best to get it out there.

That being said, the more books you have for sale, the more potential profit you will have. And the top-selling genres on Amazon, where most book sales take place*, are genre fiction—namely romance, crime, fantasy, science fiction, and inspirational. These all tend to be created as part of a series.

The amount of success you have with a stand-alone book will vary greatly, depending on each aspect of your book. Cover, quality, and genre all come into play.

FAMOUS AUTHORS WHO WROTE ONLY ONE BOOK

- Margaret Mitchell, *Gone With the Wind*
- Emily Bronte, *Wuthering Heights* (why, Emily, why?)
- Boris Pasternak, *Dr. Zhivago*
- Sylvia Plath, *The Bell Jar*

If you are working on a series and just published your first book, don't neglect your writing too much in favor of marketing book one. Your books will sell better once the series is finished. Some people will take a chance on a first book in a series without the other ones being available, but make sure you have a promise at the end for when the next book will come out.

Instead of worrying about your first book's sales, focus on building your email newsletter list, social media following, and/or blog subscribers. Then your announcement for the next book launch can be that much bigger.

- Anna Sewel, *Black Beauty*
- Ross Lockridge Jr., *Raintree Country*
- Diane Setterfield, *The Thirteenth Tale*

Although examples exist, the best method to ensure continuing sales—and establish a solid career as an author—is to publish multiple books and series over time.

THE MARKETING SANDWICH

Think about a big brand name product, like a soda brand or type of vehicle. How many kinds of ads have you seen that product featured in? Maybe on TV. A magazine ad. A billboard. Possibly even a viral video on YouTube. Why do companies advertise a product in so many different ways?

A marketing analyst named Dr. Jeffrey Lant came up with a rule of thumb many marketers recognize: the idea that a customer must be exposed to a product seven times in an 18-month period before they will purchase.

While you probably won't need to hire out billboards, it is a good idea to cover every base possible. Consider a sandwich. Bread is good, but sometimes the more complimenting ingredients you add, the better. So having an author website and your sales platforms (ie, Amazon, online retailers, and brick-and-mortar bookstores) are great places to start. But adding in a Facebook page, email newsletter, paid promotions, blog tours, ads, and other layers to your marketing will ensure that your readers simply can't miss being aware of your book.

HOW MUCH DO I HAVE TO SPEND?

You don't *have* to spend anything. Just like you can slap together a book with a pre-made CreateSpace cover and no editing for pretty much free. But the cheapest way is not the best way, especially when you're trying to stand out among millions and actually convince people to give you money in exchange for your product. Every small business requires an investment to get started, and your career as an author is no different.

There are many free ways to promote your book, but they can be extremely time-consuming. As busy moms, we know time is precious. So you have to figure out a balance that works for your budget and lifestyle.

We have three different phases of marketing strategy for each book, and different costs associated with each. The first book in a series will always need to be promoted more heavily, and the next books will rake in sales on their own thanks to your masterful writing and juicy hooks.

These phases assume that you have already established your author website, email newsletter list, and social media platforms. (If not, check out Chapter 2 or the previous book in this series, *The Busy Mom's Guide to Indie Publishing,* for detailed help in those areas.)

Here are our estimates for marketing costs for the first book in a series or a stand-alone novel (we cover these more in depth in Chapter 12):

1. **PHASE 1**, before your book comes out: $50 - $300
2. **PHASE 2**, the month your book launches: $150 - $400
3. **PHASE 3**, recurring marketing practices after launch: $50 - $300+ monthly

Now, of course these numbers will differ depending on your book's genre, how much you have to invest, and your advancement in your career. (Experienced authors can spend thousands on marketing monthly to make thousands more.) You want to have enough to make a decent start and try several different 'ingredients' for your marketing sandwich, but you don't want to just keep throwing money down an endless pit, either.

Remember, most of the money you spend will be tax-deductible. But always check with a tax professional to be sure. There are some awesome accountants out there who specialize in helping authors save moolah come tax time.

For more detail on our three marketing phases, check out Chapter 12 for a sample launch plan.

I ALREADY HAVE A BUNCH OF BOOKS OUT... BUT NO SALES. CAN THIS BOOK STILL HELP ME?

It depends. If you flip through and discover you have tried every single one of these ideas for the past few years and still have seen no sales, then you might have to face the fact that your books' niche is too small to get any traction. Or your books might need help in the editing, book cover, or back cover blurb/description department.

But we're pretty sure there's something in here that you might have overlooked or not tried yet that can boost your books with the juice they need. We're constantly stumbling across new ideas and finding new strategies and tactics to try. At the end of the day, it's the combined efforts of many different flavors that make a delicious marketing sammich.

Can you use these tips to boost a book that has been on the market for awhile? Absolutely! Angela has books that have been out for years, and when she incorporates these marketing ideas, she will see a surge in sales almost every time. It's all about getting the product in front of new eyes.

If all else fails, keep this book for next time you launch; it will most certainly help you prepare for the best release possible.

BUT I *HATE* MARKETING!

Angela hates doing the laundry. She hates doing the dishes almost as much as Jamie does. We both hate pretty much any form of housework, to be honest, and sometimes cooking too. But we both *love* having clean houses and good healthy meals.

You love writing—otherwise you wouldn't have picked up this

WHAT SHOULD I CHARGE FOR MY BOOK?

We've covered this information in *The Busy Moms Guide to Indie Publishing,* but here's a review just in case you missed it. We recommend you check out other indie books in your genre of the same length when pricing your Kindle and paperback books.

Of course, you will charge more for paperback books than Kindle books. Do not try to charge what bestselling authors with millions of fans charge for Kindle books. It's going to be very hard for an unknown indie author to make $9.99 on a 30,000-word novella for Kindle.

If you have a series, consider offering the first book for a little bit less. For example, if you have a three-book series, you might consider offering the first book for $2.99 and the other books for $4.99. You can always tweak the prices later if you need to. For more on pricing strategies, check out Chapter 11: Extreme Book Marketing.

Amazon Kindle will give you 70% in royalties if the book is priced between $2.99 and $9.99, or 35% if it is priced lower or higher than that. Also remember that you will be charged a delivery fee that varies by your book's file size if it is priced in the 70% margin.

book. We promise we'll try to make your excursions into marketing as painless as possible. After all, we've already tried all this stuff out, so we can share our best tips and at least spare you the bumps in the road and cliffs we tumbled over.

All the effort has been worth it for us and resulted in solid careers doing what we love most: writing. We have our dream job. And with the proper investment and effort, you can, too.

CAN I QUIT MY DAY JOB?

Please don't do that yet. It's really hard to tell how much you'll make month to month with your books, and that number will change constantly. Most authors that we know who make a living from writing alone have several books or series out.

You *can* make a decent living with indie books, but we suggest you set small goals at first (like bringing in enough for grocery money) and move up from there. Don't expect to make millions, or even hundreds, right away.

We promise the methods in this book will help you, but we won't promise you that new Mustang. Or even a Focus. But the more books you write, the more you improve your craft, and the more you market, the more your dreams will crystallize into reality.

QUESTIONS:

1. What was the last thing I bought because of an advertisement? How did that advertisement convince me to buy the item?
2. How much time am I willing to put into advertising every week? How can I carve that time out of my day without sacrificing too much time with my family?
3. How much can I invest each month for marketing? Could I cut back in one or two areas and use that money to make a profit?

Chapter 2

BUILDING YOUR
AUTHOR PLATFORM

"Cultivating an audience is essential to the success of any book."

— Caroline Patti

When Angela first decided to self-publish her book, it never occurred to her that she would need to build a fanbase for her books. She figured she could just put a book out there on Amazon, and people would hopefully see the cover, like it, and buy it.

But most authors, if they want to make a steady income and a stable career, have to build something called a marketing 'platform.' This is different from a distribution or sales platform like Amazon or Barnes & Noble—your marketing platform is basically a network of enthusiastic fans who love your books and will buy your newest release as soon as it comes out.

Your platform is composed of a series of online groups that you control. This includes your:

1. Website and/or blog

2.   Email newsletter
3.   Social media profiles and fan pages
4.   Street team or alpha/beta reader team
5.   Any book club dedicated to your novels, or group of people who support you

These outlets can take a while to build an audience in, but steady dedication to growing them will make each new book launch more successful than the last. Your platform is the key to bringing in predictable, dependable income for you as a writer.

YOUR AUTHOR WEBSITE & BLOG

Your website is the home base for your marketing platforms, from your blog to your to your email newsletter to your street team. Like a digital business card, your website lets readers connect with you wherever you're available, and it should provide plenty of juicy information about your books and clear direction where to buy them.

There are two major components to every website: its domain name and its hosting.

GRAB YOUR DOMAIN NAME, QUICK!

Your website's domain name is the address it lives at, such as 'jamiesfoley.com.' There's very high competition for domain names—so much so that most common English words and names have already been claimed. There are even companies that buy out tons of domain names and sit on them for years, then ransom them out for hundreds or even thousands of dollars when someone requests them.

So it's important that you grab your domain name as soon as possible, before someone else does. We recommend using your author name or pen name, or as close as you possibly can to the name that appears on your book covers.

Avoid using one of your character or series' names. There's always the chance you will branch out and write something completely different in the future. Trust us, it's easier to keep everything in one place. However, domain names are so cheap that you might choose to scoop up the name of your book or series as well and have it 'forward' to your main website.

Domain names only cost about $12 - $15 per year. The biggest name among domain name registrars is GoDaddy, but there are plenty of others to choose from that will do just fine. Jamie's personal favorite is Hover.com.

CHOOSING A WEB HOST

Your website host is like the hard drive where your website's data actually lives. Selecting a host can be a daunting task, especially since there are so many choices out there.

It's important to have a professional-looking website, but you don't have to spend an arm and a leg for this nowadays. Some writers hire a designer to build a stand-alone custom website while others opt for a free template-based website. Regardless of your choice, your priorities should be to make your website clean, eye-pleasing, and easy to navigate.

FREE TEMPLATE-BASED WEBSITES:

- **They're free!** A simple, free way to get started in a jiffy. Did we mention they're free?
- **Easy to use.** Clean web interfaces on most blog sites like Wordpress, Blogger, and Weebly are intuitive enough for even non-techies to set up and manage their own website.
- **Not-super-professional website address.** The web host's name

will be included as part of your web address. For example, Angela's free website is angelacastillowrites.weebly.com, while Jamie's custom site is jamiesfoley.com. However, some sites like Wordpress.com will let you use your own paid domain name to mask the address.

- **Stuck in template land.** Free websites are restricted to themes, so design and functionality is limited. But most popular website builders are so advanced that you'll still be able to easily create a beautiful, customized design.
- **No control over ads.** The web host may display their own ads on your website outside of your control, and you might not be able to host your own ads.

STAND-ALONE CUSTOM WEBSITES:

- **Professional website address & emails.** You can choose your own domain name, such as jamiesfoley.com. You can also get your own email address at your domain, such as billy@billybobjones.com.
- **Unlimited design.** You can design your site however you like—you're only limited by your imagination and your webmaster's ability.
- **Costly creation & hosting.** Web hosting (which is different from your domain name) runs about $115 - $130 per year. On top of that, your web designer will charge their own fee, which could run anywhere from a couple hundred to a few thousand depending on their experience.
- **Possibly complicated maintenance.** You might also have to pay a monthly fee for your website's maintenance if you don't know how to do it yourself. Ask your webmaster to teach you how to maintain your own website to save a lot of money over time. They'll still be there to bail you out when you need help.
- **A source of revenue.** You can monetize your website by signing

up for programs like Google AdSense to display ads on your website. You can also sign up for referral programs like Amazon Associates, which pays you a small percentage of purchases on Amazon to you when links on your website refer the buyer.

As a webmaster herself, Jamie recommends that every author who is just starting out get a cheap domain name and hook it up to a free blog. You don't need a flashy or high-tech website in the beginning of your career, but if you'd like to pay a freelancer to make you a beautiful custom design down the road (when your books are established and definitely profitable), you can always make that investment later.

Angela uses Weebly.com and has done so for years. It's absolutely free to use (her domain name is also free because she includes 'Weebly' in it) and she couldn't be happier with the service. They have an easy-to-use builder that includes photo gallery options and all kinds of nifty gadgets. You can also connect products to your PayPal account so people can order and pay for books from you very simply.

There are plenty of other blog platforms that also offer free website hosting and customizable templates with easy-to-use builders, including Wordpress.com and Blogger.com.

AUTHOR WEBSITE CHECKLIST:

- [ ] Email newsletter sign-up
- [ ] Progress bar for the next book
- [ ] Book pages with buy links
- [ ] Author biography
- [ ] Event schedule
- [ ] Contact page

DO I HAVE TO BLOG? I'D RATHER CLEAN OUT MY KID'S CLOSET.

No, you don't *have to* blog. But blogging is an easy way to post updates and goodies about your books—and attract and retain readership.

We recommend you post to your blog at least two or three times a month. You can post cover reveals, photograph journals, things you've learned as a writer... even funny things your kids say or do. You can also swap articles or interviews with other writers in your genre. Blog swaps mean double the content with less effort from you, and sharing your audiences will be mutually beneficial.

Content is key—not what's interesting to you, necessarily, but to your target audience. If you are writing historical fiction, for instance, you might consider including articles about characters in history from that

BLOG POST IDEAS

- Juicy behind-the-scenes details from your books
- Maps, magic system diagrams, glossaries, or appendices from your books
- Music that inspires you
- Fan art, or artwork that inspires you (thank you, Pinterest)
- Articles of interest, such as visits to the town you've written about or historical information
- Reviews of other books in your genre that you enjoy (ask your webmaster if you can monetize this with Amazon Associates)
- Funny or relevant events in your personal life, such as recaps of author events, conferences, vacations, or holidays

time period. Include recipes and interesting facts about inventions and practices during a specific era. If you write romances, you could include articles for date ideas and lists of romantic cities and/or countries. Get creative!

AUTHOR EMAIL NEWSLETTER

Many authors swear by a monthly email newsletter. It's one of the best ROI (return on investment) marketing strategies, and it allows you to reach your readers directly, exactly when you need to.

Having your own email list allows you to capture fans of your first book to ensure they hear the announcement of your second. The larger your email list grows, the more successful your next book launch will be. And the next, and the next.

If you can, start gathering sign-ups for your author newsletter even before you publish your first book. We recommend signing up for a free-until-X-amount-of-subscribers service. MailChimp is very easy to use and free until you reach 2,000 subscribers, and then it gets pretty expensive—about $50 per month. At that point, Jamie recommends MailerLite, which is almost as awesome for about half the price. Both services offer templates that are a piece of cake to put together and very clean and intuitive to use.

Having a large newsletter audience also opens you up to other newsletter opportunities, like 'newsletter swaps' with other authors. You promote a buddy in your same genre on your audience, and they in turn promote your books to their audience. Also, it's great to give reviews of other books in your genre and share them to your blog and/or newsletter. Their authors might be very thankful—especially if you have a large fan base—and thank you in turn with a kind review.

Don't stress about your open rate. Plenty of emails go to spam, or into the endless pit of someone's inbox and overlooked. A 30% open rate is considered good, and 40% is excellent. If your rate drops below 20%,

If you write more than one genre

(and they're radically different), you should consider having two separate email lists and therefore two different newsletters. This is also something to consider if you write books under separate pen names.

Why? Different genres have different target audiences. To maintain a good readership, it's best to offer each audience what most interests them. Fans of your middle-grade adventure series probably aren't interested in your erotic fiction alter-ego.

Jamie and Angela each have their own newsletters for their fiction novels, and they have a separate email list for this non-fiction series, the *Busy Mom* books. Most email services have the option to maintain multiple lists.

you might want to look into how to craft subject lines or reconsider the content of your newsletters.

Two of our favorite ways to quickly build a newsletter audience are multi-author giveaways like those hosted by BookSweeps.com and multi-author Facebook parties with giveaways for subscribers. Keep an eye out for authors in your genre who might be throwing Facebook parties for their cover reveals or book launches. By joining and supporting them, you're not only making a valuable friendship and gaining exposure to their audience, but possibly capturing their followers for your newsletter as well.

HOW DO I GET PEOPLE TO SIGN UP FOR MY NEWSLETTER?

- Offer a free short story or novella upon sign-up
- Create a contest or giveaway for new sign-ups—Amazon gift cards work as great prizes
- Put a sign-up form on your website below the progress bar for your upcoming book (if you have Wordpress, check out the free *MyBookProgress* plugin by Author Media)
- Advertise your newsletter in the backmatter of your books
- Promise regular giveaways, sales, and behind-the-scenes goodies exclusively for your newsletter subscribers

PATREON

Patreon is a relatively new website created for all types of artists, and is kind of a mash-up between a blog and a crowdfunding platform such as GoFundMe, Kickstarter, or Indiegogo. (For more detail about crowdfunding and fundraising, check out Chapter 2 of *The Busy Mom's Guide to Indie Publishing.*)

Your fans can sign up to support authors and artists in monetary increments—normally starting at $1.00 per month, or per release (chapter, short story, artwork, etc.). These pledges give supporters access to various exclusive artist-created items, such as podcasts, videos, and blog articles.

Patreon can be a fun way to share snippets of writing with your followers and perhaps bring in extra dough, but we suggest you leave this step until you've become established in other social media facets. It takes quite a bit of time and effort to cultivate a following of this nature. But the reward is sweet: dependable income on the side.

If you decide to take the Patreon plunge, we encourage you to produce a short video where you introduce yourself as an author and talk about what you write. This should be less than three minutes long— ideally around one minute. It doesn't have to be complicated; you can get a decent video with your cell phone.

PATREON LINGO

- **Patron:** Someone who has signed up to support you with a monetary pledge on your Patreon page.
- **Tiers & Rewards:** Tiers are different levels of subscription rates people will pay to support you. For example, for $1 a month you can offer access to a short article every month, or simply your undying gratitude. For $5 a month you can offer a Kindle book of their choice (from your writing). Study other writer's Patreon pages for tier reward ideas.

- **Goals:** These are bonuses you will promise subscribers when you reach a certain milestone, like an amount of monthly subscriptions or total pledge income. For example, you could promise to write a new short story if you hit $50 worth of monthly subscribers.

QUESTIONS:

1. What should my domain name be? Do I want a free website I design myself or should I hire a webmaster and have my own custom site?
2. What are some of the best, funniest, or most memorable blog posts or news articles I've read? How can I recreate this for readers of my blog?
3. Which host should I choose for my email newsletter, and is there something I can give away for free (like a short story or poem) when people sign up?

Chapter 3

SOCIAL MEDIA MANIA

*"*C*ontent is fire, social media is gasoline."*

— Jay Baer

Using social media for marketing seems like a no brainer. Everyone's on Facebook, Pinterest, Twitter, or Instagram, so it makes sense these tools are good ways to reach the masses. (As you already know if you've ever posted a picture of your child within twenty yards of some unlikely safety hazard, or a shared a shot of a kid eating anything with Red 40 food coloring.)

Facebook isn't the only social media site you could be on, but you shouldn't feel pressured to join every single social website out there. Choose one or two that you enjoy and will be consistent with. We do recommend that Facebook be one of those, but the best choices for you depend on where your readership is.

While social media can provide effective ways to get your word out (and many authors *love* them), an almost scientific approach is needed to see good results in terms of book sales. Social media platforms aren't our favorite marketing tool, but we'll go over the basics of each tool and explore the possibilities. Some of these methods will be explored more in further chapters as well.

CREATING AN AUTHOR NETWORK

Chances are, during your writing journey you have already met fantastic authors—both indie and traditional—in your same genre. Now is the time to start working with these wonderful people, both inside and outside of social media.

Ask to trade Facebook likes (this is important at the beginning when you're trying to get enough Facebook likes for your posts to show up in newsfeeds). Follow them on Instagram and Twitter and ask them to follow you back and retweet. Trade newsletter posts with writers in similar genres. Pin each other's books on your Pinterest boards.

FACEBOOK

Yes, everyone's on Facebook, but you don't want to spam unsuspecting friends and relatives with your book news every five minutes. It's a good way to have the dreaded 'unfriend' button descend upon you.

So the first thing you want to do is create a public business page, separate from your personal profile. This isn't just our suggestion to keep your ducks in a row—it's against Facebook's policies to post constant promotional content on a personal feed.

When you're creating your new Facebook page, call it something like "Your Name Author" so people can see it's different from your personal page. Then invite anyone you think would be interested in your book to like the page.

Be sure to fill out the search tags. These will direct people to your page when they type in those words on the Facebook search bar. Some good keywords to include would be 'books,' 'author,' and words relating to your genre. If someone was looking for your book, what would they search for?

You can invite anyone you want to like your page, but don't feel hurt if not everyone does. Some people don't like solicitations, some don't read, and a few—gasp—just don't ever read notifications.

Unfortunately, having a page also means that your posts won't naturally be seen by people who have liked it. This is because if Facebook gave the same weight to every business's posts, everyone's feeds would be full of ads, and people would leave the platform. So in order to ensure that a post is seen by as many people as possible, it will need to be 'boosted' with cold, hard cash. We recommend only boosting your most popular posts—or the most important ones—for just a few dollars when needed.

FACEBOOK GROUPS

If you run a search for 'Kindle book' on Facebook, you will find hundreds of pages and groups with names like 'Great Ebooks for You' and 'Kindle Bargain Hunters.'

These groups have been set up to be matchmakers for authors and readers. Authors are free to post links to their books on Amazon, and readers are able to find books in their genre that they might want to read.

The majority of these groups or pages are set up specifically for free or discounted Kindle books, and they're free for you as an author to participate in. So when you set up a promotional day for your Kindle book where you will be offering it for free or at a discount (more on that later!), utilizing these sites can be very effective.

Search for groups that target your genre's audience specifically. Some of these groups may be smaller, but your book will have a better chance of being seen by someone who is specifically looking for that genre.

We suggest you create an eye-catching graphic with your book's cover, buy link, and amount the book is selling for. And perhaps even a quote from the book or a line from the blurb. You can post this graphic to the Facebook groups along with an excerpt from the book or more from the blurb in your post.

This can be time-consuming, so it's a good idea to research the best days and times of the day to post. Angela tries to post hers between 2pm and 5pm in the afternoon on weekdays. If the baby is taking a nap.

Also—and this is *very* important—be sure to read each Facebook group's guidelines *before* you post. Some groups only allow you to post about promotions during certain days, and/or have restrictions for certain genres.

TWITTER

Twitter can be helpful, especially if you love to share tidbits that are funny, inspirational, or news-oriented. But you have to build up a huge following and maintain it, since tweets come and go in mere seconds.

Band together with other authors and agree to trade 'retweeting' posts to your followers. If you have 10 authors who 'retweet' to 500 followers each, you will have 5000 followers reached in moments. This is another reason why networking with other authors is very important.

Don't forget the power of hashtags. #indieauthor, #indiebooks, #ebooks and #bookaddict are good ones. However, be careful. If you use irrelevant hashtags that have nothing to do with your post just because they are trendy, you can get banned from Twitter. And nobody wants that.

Most authors who use Twitter on a regular basis agree that you have to stay on top of it. So this means tweeting and retweeting several times a day, carefully following people and unfollowing those who don't follow you back, and generally a lot of maintenance. But it can also be a lot of fun.

PINTEREST

Pinterest can be a great tool for research and inspiration before you publish your book, and an interactive way to gain readers' interest. You can create boards with costume ideas, stories about a specific country or time period, even pictures of models who look like your character. Invite people to share pins that might be helpful.

When your book is published, make sure you pin it to your author board. Get creative. For example, make a 'top ten' list of books in your genre and add your book to the list. Create a board for other indie authors and trade pins with them. Make topic-themed boards with specific commonalities, like 'books with dragons,' 'romances with Navy SEALs,' or 'books with Amish vampires in space.' (Yes, that's a real book—Jamie knows the author. Ha!)

Pinterest is also a good way to share specific blog posts and giveaways (just remember to remove the post when the giveaway has expired), and especially anything you have unique art for. Pinterest users are almost exclusively women, who tend to be aged around 20-30. Keep that in mind when deciding which platform to use—you need to be posting wherever your audience is.

INSTAGRAM

Photo-driven books, such as cookbooks and children's books, do well with a photo-driven social concept like Instagram. However, any exposure is good exposure, and many authors have found ways to use Instagram for marketing. One of these ways is to work with other writers—especially bloggers who have large followings.

Instagram is another good way to have readers interact with your writing journey. Share pictures of places you've gone to research your book (for example, Angela posted pictures of pioneer farms she toured when researching *The River Girl's Song*), or recipes and foods that might be featured in your book. Take pictures when you get your first paperback proofs and of people reading your books. Share pictures of fun bookish decorations, library ladders, free libraries ... whatever keeps people following and interested, as long as it's aesthetically pleasing.

You can also connect your Instagram account with the Facebook ads manager to advertise with them both. Hashtags don't jive very well with Facebook, but they're all the rage on Instagram. Try using #bookstagram for book lovers, and find hashtags for anything related to the content of your post.

OTHER SOCIAL MEDIA SITES YOU CAN USE (BUT LET'S BE REAL—WHO HAS TIME FOR ALL THAT?)

- Tumblr
- Snapchat
- YouTube
- Google+
- Stumbleupon
- LinkedIn
- Anchor
- Medium
- Wanelo

GOODREADS

Owned by Amazon, Goodreads is like a digital library that your books are sure to appear on at one point or another. Create your author page and claim your books. Many avid readers have Goodreads as their home base, so having a robust profile can increase your books' visibility with the right crowd.

You can make friends on Goodreads, hook it up to your blog, respond to questions from your readers, browse groups and forums, and more. But the biggest feature Goodreads is known for—and hated for—is book reviews.

Reviews on Goodreads tend to be harsher than most, and part of that has to do with its rating system (we'll cover this in the next chapter). Regardless, Goodreads is a book-centric platform that every author should definitely be a part of.

AMAZON & BOOKBUB FOLLOWERS

When people follow your Amazon and BookBub pages, it's similar to getting Facebook page likes. The cool thing about these is when you have a new book release, both Amazon and BookBub will notify the folks who follow you. Sweet!

BookBub followers will multiply if/when you land one of their deals (which can take a while). Amazon will not tell you how many followers you have on your page (and there is no way to find out), but it's nice to have them for release days.

There are a few ways you can gain followers. Set up a contest (see Chapter 8: Magical Unicorn Giveaways) and make following you on Amazon or BookBub one of the ways people can enter. You can also add a link to your newsletters suggesting people follow you. There are a few promotional services such as Authors Cross Promotion and BookSweeps that can help you garner more BookBub followers. You can also host public Amazon Giveaways where you can make following you a requirement for entry.

THUNDERCLAP

Thunderclap is a free service authors can use to engage more of an audience for a specific event, like a book release. Thunderclap uses an online tool to release a tweet, post to Facebook, and send a Tumblr message to as many people as agree to support you. The basic service costs nothing, but you must get at least 100 people to sign up. Anyone who has all three accounts can support you in all three ways.

Several Facebook groups are dedicated to authors who trade Thunderclap support, and you can also ask fans on your author page. Don't ask too often, or it becomes another form of spam.

Thunderclaps can be effective, but it's good to really think through your message and make sure you have the support needed in the time given. Otherwise it's a lot of work and not much of a thunder … clap.

WHAT DO I POST TO MY SOCIAL MEDIA PAGES?

We recommend you post something at least once a day, but it should only be a sales pitch every seventh post or less. Don't break this rule or you'll lose followers faster than a snake-oil salesman.

Your posts should be catered to your audience, and to what would interest them specifically. If you write young adult fiction, post funny memes.If you write in the Christian genres, post verses or inspirational quotes. If you write political commentary, post your thoughts on news stories.

Or you could post an interesting article related to your research, or a simple GIF or meme related to reading or writing. Interactive posts are great ways to get people to comment with their favorite books, genre, fictional characters, etc. What catches your attention on Facebook? Find funny videos on YouTube to share. Anything that's still connected to the subject at hand—your genre.

Try to make sure every post has a picture or video included; as people are more likely to engage with a post that has an image of some kind, and some social media sites like Facebook will rank them higher on your followers' feeds.

This is a fun way to include your children (if the books are family-friendly). Have one of your children dress up as your main character, or draw a picture of what they think they look like. If you've written a children's story or a book for middle-grade readers, get a picture of you reading your story to your kids. Post your children's thoughts about your book (they're probably going to be hilarious 90% of the time).

Facebook writers' groups and Pinterest have oodles of quotes, lists, and articles that are free (and encouraged) to be shared. You can also create your own memes with a basic graphics program (Canva is one free online tool). Choose a pretty landscape picture from your own photos or grab a free one from a free photo site like Unsplash (*please* make sure it's free before you use it). Find an interesting quote and add it on. Pick a cool line from your story to add, and be sure to make sure you give yourself (and your book) credit in the body of the meme.

BALANCING SOCIAL MEDIA WHILE STILL HAVING A LIFE

Blog articles, newsletter stories, Facebook posts, website content, Instagram photos … how often and how much? Here's a one-glance list to help you prioritize, but remember, most authors will not keep up with all of this. Just do your best—even a minimal effort in these areas is better than nothing. And if something brings in a ton of interest while the other is a bit lackluster, by all means, focus on what works for you.

ONCE OR TWICE A WEEK:
- Post something interesting on Facebook related to your genre, writing, or books

- Tweet or retweet something on Twitter
- Repin a few pins to your Pinterest boards
- Post an attractive picture to Instagram

TWO TO FOUR TIMES A MONTH:
- Post a blog article
- Visit Facebook groups related to your genre

ONCE A MONTH:
- Send out an email newsletter
- Check up on your Goodreads page

QUESTIONS:

1. Which social media platforms should I focus on? Which might I actually keep up with consistently—and enjoy it?
2. What's my favorite type of post, and what are bestselling authors in my genre posting? How can I use something similar to attract interest for my books?
3. What unique Pinterest boards can I create to get more readers to interact with my books?

Chapter 4

REVIEWS, TROLLS,
AND TURKISH DELIGHT

*"Personally, I am very fond of strawberries
and cream, but I have found that for
some strange reason, fish prefer worms."*

— Dale Carnegie

Book sales and reviews can seem like a chicken and egg cycle. You need reviews to make sales, but you need readers (and therefore sales) to get reviews.

If you are new to selling books, you probably haven't even considered reviews beyond the terrifying thought of others judging your work. Regardless of what others say about your work, it seems to cut to the soul—either like rat poison or Turkish delight.

Nevertheless, reviews are absolutely crucial to the effectiveness of your marketing, and to your book's long-term success. Or if you already have several published books in the marketplace, then you know how hard it is to get people to take that 30 extra seconds to leave their opinion.

In this chapter we'll give you advice on how to deal with good, bad, and ugly reviews, and our tried-and-true methods for racking them up.

WHY REVIEWS ARE SO IMPORTANT

There are two main reasons why gathering reviews is crucial to your books' long-term success. It's great to have plenty of reviews on all kinds of websites—from Goodreads to Barnes & Noble to Books-A-Million—but positive reviews will do you the most good on Amazon.com, where the vast majority of book sales take place.*

1. MOST READERS PAY ATTENTION TO REVIEWS

Consider a new restaurant in town. You might be an adventurous soul, and not mind plunking fifteen dollars down for food in an eatery you've never sampled. But if you're like most people, you'll ask around and see if other folks have tried the place. You might even check online reviews. If consumers have a way to find out other people's opinions, they will seek them out.

Now think about what you listen for when people tell you about a new restaurant. "We liked the atmosphere." "The food was great." "The portions are huge." These details may or may not be things you care about. Or maybe you trust one person's judgement over another. Regardless, you're much more likely to visit one place over another if it has a ton of awesome reviews.

There are *millions* of books on Amazon to choose from. And if a reader has six books lined up on the screen, all of the same genre with similar covers, then he or she is probably going to check the star rating to see which one has been enjoyed by the most readers.

2. MANY PROMO SITES REQUIRE REVIEWS

We'll get into more information about promotional websites in the next chapter, but most of the best sites require a specific number of reviews and a certain rating percentage as well. The reason is because the readers who subscribe to these sites trust that they will feature quality books. Since the promo sites don't have the time to read entire books before featuring them, they will go by public opinion.

Some sites will feature new releases if the books have professional covers and appear to be edited well, and these are good places to advertise when you're first launching your book, but eventually you will want to apply for the better sites because they bring in more sales.

DEALING WITH GOOD, BAD, AND UGLY REVIEWS

WHAT RANKINGS REALLY MEAN: AMAZON VS GOODREADS

You will probably feel anxious when you read your first reviews. Combined, our books have hundreds of reviews and even so, our palms still get sweaty when we notice a new review has been posted on one of them. No one likes to be criticized, so it's a huge relief when we see four or five gold stars winking back at us.

Keep in mind: Amazon's review system is different from Goodreads. Here's Amazon's review system as presented to readers:

1 = I hated it
2 = I didn't like it
3 = It was OK (but still counted as a 'critical review')
4 = I liked it
5 = I loved it

Goodreads has a slightly different review system, so you can expect your rating percentage to be slightly lower. Some writers choose to ignore their Goodreads ranking altogether, because unfortunately the website is notorious for critical readers and trolls.

Goodreads' system for rankings is laid out like this:

1 = Did not like it
2 = It was OK
3 = Liked it
4 = Really liked it
5 = It was amazing

BAD REVIEWS

Cue the violin music. We hate to be the bearers of bad tidings, but

DON'T FEED THE TROLLS

No matter what, don't reply to negative reviews. This is considered bad form and will make you look like a little kid throwing a temper tantrum, *even if you're right.*

If you really feel strongly about a negative review, you can ask other people to vote it as 'unhelpful.' This means if you have multiple reviews, it will show up lower down in the list and might not be seen as often. But unfortunately... it will still be there.

The only time we ever suggest replying to a negative review is if they are complaining about a formatting issue that has since been resolved.

no matter how fabulous of a writer you are, you *will* collect a few bad reviews over time. We are very sorry and we wish it weren't true, but it's going to happen.

Sometimes critical reviews can be helpful, pointing out issues that can help us improve our writing craft or plot development. And others are just plain crazy.

Angela has had one-star reviews that say "Loved it!" (you can find them if you look at her books). Some of Jamie's critical reviews are so out of left field that she's not sure they even read the same book they reviewed. And some of our favorite reviews are scathing diatribes that try to sound worthy of *The New York Times* but are riddled with spelling and grammar issues.

And people wonder why some writers become reclusive hermits who live on Chinese food delivery. (Oh man. Must. Have. Egg rolls).

Why do people leave bad reviews? Some people are irritating know-it-alls who simply feel more important criticizing everyone and putting them down. We refer to them as 'trolls.'

Sometimes critical reviewers mostly liked your book, but misread the blurb and thought it was something it wasn't. (For example, Angela receives reviews from annoyed readers who wanted more romance, even though she doesn't advertise her books as true romances).

Or sometimes readers leave the *wrong* review for a *different* book, which is fine because most of the time people reading those reviews will realize what has happened and ignore them.

And then there are those times when the reader simply did not enjoy the book. Does everyone like country music? Does everyone like polka? Yodeling? Does every kid love macaroni and cheese? Broccoli?

At these times, oh fellow tender-hearted writers, we brush away a tear from the corner of our eye and murmur, "Not our target audience."

SPOILER ALERT!

Sometimes readers leave gushing, glowing, several-paragraph

reviews about how much they adored a story, but as we are reading blithely through them, patting ourselves on the back, we realize with horror they have given away a pivotal plot point.

If this happens, you can do one of two things. If they are on Goodreads, you can contact them and *very politely* ask them to consider putting a 'spoiler alert' at the beginning of their review. The only way to contact an Amazon reviewer would be if they have an email address on their profile, but that's rare.

They may or may not comply. Or you can wait and pray that the review will get buried under a heap of more four and five star reviews and therefore become lost in the mix.

You can also try reporting the review to Amazon, but we can say from experience there is not a very high chance it will be removed. If you do try, be sure to include the link to the review in question and why

5 REASONS WHY AMAZON MAY REMOVE BAD REVIEWS

Yes, some people will experience a magical unicorn moment and get bad reviews removed. But this is very rare.

Here are the five official reasons Amazon will consider removing a review:

1. Inappropriate Content

2. Hate Speech & Offensive Content

3. One-Word Reviews

4. Promotion of Illegal Content

5. Promotional Reviews

So you can try contacting Amazon Customer Support and stating your case, but there is no guarantee.

you think it should be removed.

WHEN BAD REVIEWS CAN BE GOOD THINGS

Sometimes, when the sting has faded a bit, we can step back and find a few bright spots in the midst of the gloom that is a bad review. Here are a few things to consider:

1. **Your advertising may be a little off.** Maybe your blurb or description hinted at something the customer was hoping for but didn't find in the book. Check your product information and keywords carefully to make sure you aren't promising something that the story doesn't deliver.
2. **You can learn from it.** Several reviews complaining about the same issue can reveal what might not work for your readers. It may be a hard pill to swallow, but learning what readers don't like—and what they really want—can help you craft your next novel that much better.
3. **Editing might be an issue.** Are a lot of your customers complaining about typos? You might need to pay for another once-over by an editor and discreetly re-upload your book.
4. **Formatting errors can be super annoying.** Does your ebook appear in an unappealing way on their e-reader? This can be really frustrating for voracious readers. Consider getting your book re-formatted.
5. **Mean or dumb reviews can help sell your book.** Sometimes a review can highlight something another customer is looking for. For example, someone could post a one-star review of a historical novel saying "Too much history." (No, this is not a stretch. This sort of thing happens all the time.) Most customers will simply read this, roll their eyes and think, "That's exactly why I *want* to read it!"

HOW TO GET REVIEWS

Authors have been wrestling with their review count since the first Amazon Kindle book was published. You'd think everyone would rate every book, right? Or at least your books because they're awesome.

But think about it. Have you reviewed every book you ever read? Probably not. And unfortunately, your average reader hasn't, either.

So you need to prepare for a low review-to-sales ratio. It's just the way it is.

Angela has noticed for most of her books that she will receive, on average, one review for every 100 sales, or lower when she is promoting certain books for free with the KDP Select program (more on that in Chapter 6). Jamie sees a similar ratio.

After hearing this, gathering reviews seems like a daunting task. Like when your child brings home a sales contest slip from school and proudly announces they want the biggest prize, and therefore must sell 500 cans of stale popcorn.

But we're here to help. (Except for the popcorn part. You're on your own with that one.)

YOUR BETA READERS OR STREET TEAM

You have a beta reader team or street team, right? Right? (You should if you read the first book in this series, *The Busy Mom's Guide to Writing*. Hey, we're just trying to help.)

The best way to ensure swift, enthusiastic reviews for your books over the course of your career is to have a team of beta readers. You give them access to your manuscript before it's published, and in exchange, they give you valuable feedback and their honest reviews on your book's launch day. And because they're your biggest fans, their honesty is almost always going to be positive.

After they lend you a hand, be sure to gift them some swag, a thank-you note, and a first-edition copy of your book. They spent a lot of their precious time helping you, after all—and wouldn't it be great if they also decided to help with your next release?

GETTING REVIEWS FOR LAUNCH DAY

Amazon won't let anyone post a review before the book is up for sale. But you can get around this by releasing your paperback version a few days before the Kindle launch day (trust us, very few people will notice). Amazon will automatically link up your paperback page and Kindle page, so reviews on the paperback edition will also populate on your Kindle page.

Then send an email to your beta readers, ARC reviewers, or your street team with a link to your paperback listing. Ask them, very kindly and only once, to post their honest reviews so you'll have a jump-start on launch day.

Please note: This will not show up as a 'verified purchase,' but it's still worth having them up on launch day. If you really want verified reviews, your team will have to purchase Kindle copies straight from Amazon. Copies you gift through Amazon will still not count as verified.

WORD OF MOUTH—EXCEPT AUNT SUZIE

You might think you can just pass out copies of books to friends and family and get them to post reviews. Well, this might work, to an extent. But there are two big problems with this strategy:

1. **Aunt Suzie isn't in your target audience. And she doesn't even like to read.** We have found that it's much harder to get friends and family to read our books than we ever thought.

As hurtful as that can be, it's true. And even the friends who take the time to read our books don't always review them. You can't go around every day bugging people to leave reviews—you'll lose friends. And people will avoid sitting next to you at Thanksgiving. (Granted, that may or may not be a good thing.)

2. **Amazon has eyes everywhere.** Amazon does not approve of reviews from biased sources, and they have mysterious ways of finding out if you are directly connected to someone. Maybe you have the same last name or live in the same town. Especially if your brother writes, "This is my sister's book and you'd better read it, or else." If Amazon even *thinks* you might be connected to someone personally, they will remove the review. If this happens too often, you might even get banned from Amazon forever. Dun dun duuun!

But it's not all bad news. There are still plenty of ways that good old-fashioned word of mouth can help you score reviews.

Consider your audience. Is your book for young adults? Children? Veterans? Soccer moms? Find a group of these folks and ask if they will read and review your book. Book clubs still exist, and they're awesome. So are activity centers, libraries, and religious groups.

You can order paperbacks for them to review or see if they will accept a digital copy. Most people can pull up a Word Document or PDF file and read it on their phone just like a Kindle book. Ask them to mention in their review that they received the book for free in exchange for their honest thoughts.

BLOGGERS

There are hundreds of 'book bloggers' who love to read books and write about the books they've read. They make awesome reviewers for several reasons: many of them do it quickly and professionally, they give in-depth thoughts, and they might post their review in multiple places (like Amazon.com, BarnesAndNoble.com, and/or Goodreads.com in addition to their own blog). If they've got a large blog following, it can mean excellent exposure for your novel.

At least a month before your book launches (three months in advance is best), contact at least twenty of these bloggers and ask if they would like an Advance Reader Copy (ARC) of your book in exchange for an honest review.

The Indie View* has a long list to help you get started with finding bloggers. Or you could simply use a search engine and type in the genre of your book and 'book blogger.' For example, try searching for 'romantic suspense book blogs.'

There are thousands—or maybe even hundreds of thousands—of review blogs out there, so you'll get burned out fast if you try to contact every single one of them. Consider judging the size of their audience first. You can normally get a good idea of how large their following is by how many comments are on their posts. Or you can check their internet ranking for free at www.alexa.com.

Here are a few things to consider before going off to contact 5,000 book bloggers:

1. **Send a personalized email.** Address the blogger by name and tell them something you like about their blog. Tell them why you think your book would be a good fit for their blog. Be sincere.

2. **The demand is high.** There are hundreds of other writers out there who have discovered the same thing we have: they need reviews to make sales. And they also use the strategy of asking bloggers for reviews. So don't be offended if it takes a little time to hear back from bloggers, and don't get your feelings hurt if they politely decline. It probably just means their to-be-read stack is too high.

3. **Find out if the reviewer will accept digital copies,** and make sure you send the book in the format they request. If they absolutely insist on paperback, make sure they are in the same

country as you, or shipping could get pricey. We don't like to send paperbacks unless we're very confident that they'll follow through, and/or they have a large following to make the risk worth it.

4. **If you send a paperback copy,** write 'Proof, not for resale' inside the back cover. This means that they won't be as likely to re-sell your book on Amazon. Most bloggers aren't going to do this, but a few do try to profit from these kinds of ventures.

5. **Make sure the bloggers post their reviews to Amazon.** Some bloggers make it a policy to only post reviews to their blogs, which is still a good thing if they've got a large following. Even if it's a tiny blog with a very few subscribers, it's worth the trouble to send the book if you get an honest Amazon review.

GOODREADS

Goodreads can be an invaluable resource for writers. It's book review central, and another great place to find people who are willing to review your book. But remember, anyone you give a free copy to must say they received a complimentary copy if they post their review to Amazon.

1. **Host a giveaway.** It used to be free to do this, now Goodreads charges a pretty hefty sum (at the time of this book's publication, $119) to do it. If you do try this out, we recommend choosing the Kindle giveaway option. If you do go with paperbacks, make sure you specify you will only send to your country of origin, otherwise you might spend a fortune on shipping. It has been our experience—though there is no guarantee—that you will average 1-2 reviews for every 10 paperback books you give away in this manner. Please note: we haven't tried these giveaways since Goodreads started charging for them, but word from other indies has been that it just isn't worth the money.

2. **Goodreads forums.** Goodreads is full of voracious readers. If you do a search, you'll be able to find several groups with people willing to read free books in exchange for an honest review. You can also find groups that are essentially online book clubs for your specific genre.

3. **Search for other books like yours.** If you can find bestsellers in your genre, they're sure to have dozens of enthusiastic reviews. If your book is similar enough, they just might enjoy it, too. You don't want to privately message a hundred people and get flagged for spamming, but if you reply to their review with a comment and start a genuine conversation and friendship with them, they may be willing to review your book next. Being active in the Goodreads community can go a long way.

FACEBOOK GROUPS

A quick search on Facebook will give you dozens of groups and pages for people who love books. A little more of a specific search will bring up groups and pages of people who like your specific genre of book. Score!

It's very possible to find people who will read your book in exchange for an honest review in these types of groups. Just make sure you read the page policies before you post your request. Many groups will allow you to post a link to your book and offer free copies for honest reviews—as long as you follow their rules.

PAID REVIEW SERVICES

You might come across services that offer to post Amazon reviews for your book for a fee. *Don't fall for this!*

It's against Amazon's Terms of Service to compensate someone

Mystery
OF THE MISSING REVIEWS

One of the most frustrating things as an author with books on Amazon is when you work really, really hard to build reviews and things don't go as planned. You finally reach that seemingly unattainable number to submit to a certain promo site you've had your eye on, only to find out some of those hard-earned reviews have mysteriously vanished.

Yes, really—reviews on Amazon will occasionally just disappear.

Unless they're bad reviews, it's like a punch in the gut, and there's really nothing you can do about it. At least we can share with you a few of the reasons why Amazon removes reviews (but let's face it, some will always remain a mystery).

- **They found a connection between you and the reviewer.** Facebook friends, relatives, your pizza delivery guy... we don't know how they know, but they know.
- **Review swaps.** If you've swapped reviews with another author, you might get those reviews removed—and even could be reprimanded.
- **Amazon figured out you paid for the reviews from a service.** This includes gift cards and free books—you can give a free book for a review request, but you cannot require a review.
- **The review contained something against Amazon's TOS.** Reviews that contain prohibited information, like phone numbers, links to products, or harmful content are likely to be removed.

directly—other than offering a free sample—to review your product. We have heard horror stories from authors who fell for these sales pitches and were subsequently banned from putting books on Amazon. Forever.

However, you can pay a matchmaking service that will hook you up with readers willing to leave *honest* reviews in exchange for a free copy of your book.

Services such as NetGalley, Story Cartel, eBook Discovery's Read & Review program, and Authors Cross Promotion offer your book to people in the *hopes* that they will leave a review. You are paying for them to present your book to this audience of reviewers, and nothing else. There are other options like these available that are perfectly fine according to Amazon's Terms of Service, but please do your homework before using them.

Beware NetGalley, which is the largest review service used by publishers, so it's very expensive. While they can generate a large amount of reviews for you, their reviewers are notorious for being overly critical and even vicious.

PATIENCE

Place a note at the end of your paperbacks and ebooks asking for an honest review. When you sell a book to someone at a book signing, tell them you'd love to hear their honest thoughts in an Amazon.com review.

The majority of reviews will trickle in as your books sell more and more copies over time. So part of the process means being patient. Not our favorite thing, but it's part of the journey. And it pays off!

LANDING EDITORIAL REVIEWS

Some services, such as Kirkus Reviews, Publisher's Weekly, Library Journal, and Readers' Favorite, will charge for giving your book one honest review. This won't appear as a normal review on Amazon—it's special.

You can use editorial reviews for listing in the front of your book, the Editorial Reviews section on your Amazon book page, or choose a snippet from the snazziest one to put on your cover.

With the exception of Readers' Favorite (which is free unless you pay them to do it quickly), these reviewers tend to be very expensive. They promise an in-depth, honest review and publish it on their website or in a periodical.

Please note: a paid review doesn't necessarily mean a *good* review. We know some folks who have been reamed by Kirkus and Publisher's Weekly. Reader's Favorite tends to be positive, though, so give their free service a shot.

QUESTIONS:

1. Which of these suggestions can I try first to collect reviews? What can I afford more of—time or money—and would some options be better to pursue after I've finished a series?
2. How am I going to prepare myself for negative reviews? Is there a place I can display my favorite positive reviews for encouragement?
3. What local places—such as bookstores, libraries, clubs, and activity centers—can I become involved with to garner long-term support for my books?

Chapter 5

PAID PROMOTIONS:
AN INDIE'S BREAD AND BUTTER

"   ... The work of promoting the book requires just as much work as writing the book, if not more so."

— Adam S. McHugh

Large companies can spend around a billion dollars every year on advertising. So it makes sense to assume that if you pay to promote something, you should see sales and return on your investment.

But sometimes promotions don't work. Consider the disastrous 'MagiCan' Coca-Cola promotion in 1990. The company developed these cool cans that would spit out money—up to $500—when you opened the can. The problem was, they had to balance the cans with water so no one could tell which cans held the prizes.

And the water leaked. So when people did find the amazing money cans, they had nasty, moldy money inside.*

This was, at the time, the most expensive promotion the company had ever done, but because of all the complaints they had to pull 300,000 of the 500,000 'MagiCans' off the shelves. Hey, if you asked us, moldy money is better than no money, but we digress.

We learn from instances like this—and from questionable yet wildly successful marketing campaigns like the Chick-fil-A cows, the "Wassup" Budweiser commercial, or the 'Got Milk?' moustaches—that the trick to marketing is not necessarily how much you spend, but where you put your dollars.

(Great. Now we're going to answer every phone call for the next week with, *"Wassaaaaaaaaaaap?"*)

FIND YOUR NICHE

In the days of yore, when Angela started marketing her very first *Toby the Trilby* book in 2013, she had no idea how the whole Amazon thing worked. She thought most customers would still be purchasing paperbacks.

To her surprise, as books began to sell, the majority were purchased from Kindle. Her Kindle books outsold her paperback books about 50:1. Angela still liked having the paperback options to sell at local events and to family and friends, but she didn't sell many physical books to online customers.

Of course, there are always exceptions. Picture books, workbooks, and art books might sell more paperback copies. Angela is part of an anthology *(Steampunk Fairy Tales Volume I)* which is available on Amazon Kindle for free, but amazingly, she sells dozens of paperbacks every month. That's why we always recommend having both versions of your book available for sale.

Many Kindle readers have voracious appetites and will gobble up every book in their chosen genre. So the key is to get a story into their hands, capture their email addresses for your email newsletter, and continue writing new stories to sell to these people.

These are the readers who will go to library book sales and buy baskets full of paperbacks—it's the equivalent to binge watching entire seasons of shows on Netflix. *These people exist in droves, and they are a writer's best friends.* You simply have to find a way to reach them.

For our books, which are mostly genre fiction like romances, historicals, contemporaries, and science fiction and fantasy, one of the best methods to reach our readers—and our income goals—is free pulsing our books with promotional websites.

We call our favorite marketing method free pulsing: offering a Kindle book for free on one day to generate sales the next day, sell the rest of the books in the series, and rack up Pages Read in the Kindle Unlimited program. We pay a promotional website to feature our book for free on that day to their subscribers, and make the money back in books sales.

Yes, it sounds crazy. But it works, and we'll explain it all in the next chapter.

If the idea of offering your book for free is abhorrent, many promo sites will feature deals of your book priced at discounts—normally for $0.99 and not exceeding $2.99. Discounted books just don't make us as much moolah as free pulsing promotions, in our experience.

HOW DO PROMO SITES WORK?

Most book promotion websites run under the concept that people want cheap books. So they collect subscribers by asking for email sign-ups. The best promo sites have e-mail lists by the thousands (or hundreds of thousands), and they send emails offering links to free or discounted books several times a week.

Some of these sites have subscribers for preferred genres, so they only receive book offers in those categories, while others send out all the offers at once in one big jumbled email.

Many of these sites also send out a blast throughout several social media platforms, as well as a feature on their own website. So they utilize Facebook, Twitter, their website, and email to share your book deal with as many readers as possible.

GETTING ACCEPTED FOR A PROMOTION

Promo sites won't market just any book. Most of them have gatekeepers—people on staff who choose which books are best for their readership, and *Underwater Basket Weaving, Fifth Edition* might not make the cut. Unless it has a hundred 5-star reviews and a cover that belongs in an art gallery.

In the last chapter about reviews, we discussed how important reviews are to landing promotions. When you begin scoping out promo sites, you will find that many of the best ones have requirements for books they promote. Most of them require:

1. A professional-looking cover (in other words, something a little better than your five-year-old could put together)
2. Well-edited content
3. No offensive content (it depends—some sites are fine with erotica and horror, just check the guidelines)
4. 5-10 Amazon.com reviews (some can require as many as 50)
5. 3.5+ Amazon.com average review rating (some require a rating of 4.0+ stars).

Read the submission requirements carefully. Some sites will allow you to promote a new release that has no or few reviews, because they understand a new book takes time to garner reviews. They're even more likely to feature a new release if you already have other awesome books under your belt that you can point them to.

What if you've done your best but still don't have any reviews?

Well, we all have to start somewhere. You can still look into smaller promo sites like bknights on Fiverr which only costs $6 for an ad or Bookscream to get you started. You can also use social media (which we cover in Chapter 2), pay-per-click ads (Chapter 7), or giveaways (Chapter 8) to help you get the word out and get reviews trickling in over time.

PLEASE DON'T SPEND A MILLION DOLLARS

As you are exploring the internet cosmos, you're going to find some extremely pricey promotional sites. Some places charge $500 or more and promise you the moon. And stars. And figgy pudding.

Throwing your money at a promo site will not always make you a millionaire (in fact—shocker—it normally won't). We suggest you start small, with your promo site budget set at $50 or less per month, and invest more money as you discover which sites work for your book and see the sales start to grow.

GENRE MATTERS

Some promo sites charge a flat rate for any genre you submit to while others charge different prices for different genres. Why?

Because while they might have 11,000 readers signed up to receive offers for historic romance, they could have 50,000 readers signed up for cozy mysteries. So it might be five times the price, but your book will be offered to five times as many people.

If your book could fit into two different genres, you will have to decide if you want to spend less money and reach fewer people, or spend more and reach more. When trying out a new site, we recommend spending less at first. Some sites also allow you to promote your book to more than one of their genre email lists, and it will take some testing to figure out if this works for you.

While we're on the subject of genres—and this might already be obvious—your book might do better at one promotional website than another, simply because of genre. Some websites perform better for Angela's books than Jamie's, and vice versa. Their readership might generally prefer a certain type of book depending on how that promo site acquired and built their audience.

In fact, certain sites will only take specific genres. Book Barbarian, for instance, only takes fantasy and sci-fi. My Book Cave refuses to advertise anything of an erotic nature. Many of Angela's favorite promo sites only advertise clean books to their Christian audience—another good reason to read every promo site's guidelines carefully before submitting.

PROMO SITES WORTH USING

Here's a list of book promotion sites we have used consistently and almost always made a profit.

PLEASE NOTE: We are not guaranteeing these sites will work for your book or that they will give you a reasonable return on your investment. Unfortunately, just because they tend work for our books doesn't mean they'll work for yours (or ours either if it's an off season or holiday where people don't want to read as much as normal, if we've used the site too frequently, or if our kids all wake up on the wrong side of the bed and it's just an off day).

Notice that we have not added submission info or pricing—this is because they constantly changing. Please check each site for updated information, and test them independently before throwing the big bucks at them.

OUR FAVORITES (HIGHEST RETURN ON INVESTMENT):

1. BookBub: http://bookbub.com
2. My Book Cave: https://mybookcave.com
3. Robin Reads (especially the 'Featured' slot): http://robinreads.com
4. Ebook Discovery: https://ebookdiscovery.com
5. Bknights (through Fiverr): https://www.fiverr.com/bknights
6. Book Barbarian (Sci-fi and fantasy books only): http://bookbarbarian.com

AVERAGE RESULTS (NORMALLY DECENT RETURN ON INVESTMENT):

1. Ereader News Today http://ereadernewstoday.com
2. Many Books: http://manybooks.net
3. Fussy Librarian: http://www.thefussylibrarian.com
4. The E-reader Cafe: https://theereadercafe.com
5. Book Runes: http://bookrunes.com
6. Book Raid: http://www.bookraid.com
7. Faithful Reads (Christian books only): https://faithfulreads.com
8. Spirit-Filled Kindle (Christian books only): http://spiritfilledebooks.com

MIXED RESULTS (USE AT YOUR OWN RISK):

1. Book Lemur: https://www.booklemur.com
2. Book Gorilla: http://www.bookgorilla.com
3. Book Shark: http://www.bookshark.com
4. BookSends: http://www.booksends.com
5. EreaderIQ: http://www.ereaderiq.com
6. Bookwerm: http://www.bookwerm.com
7. KND (Kindle Nation Daily): http://kindlenationdaily.com

8. FKBT (Free Kindle Books and Tips): http://fkbt.com
9. justkindlebooks: http://www.justkindlebooks.com
10. Ebook Hounds: http://www.ebookhounds.com
11. YourNewBooks: http://www.yournewbooks.com
12. Freebooksy: https://www.freebooksy.com
13. The Books & The Bear: http://booksandthebear.com
14. Books Butterfly: http://booksbutterfly.com

BOOKBUB: THE KING OF THE JUNGLE

If you bring up promotions to indies, eventually BookBub will enter the conversation. Why? BookBub is the absolute Promo King.

While some other promo sites have decent subscriber lists of several hundred thousand, Bookbub has *millions*. They charge anywhere from $80 to feature middle-grade fiction to $500+ for crime. (These prices are for promoting books on free days—the charge goes up for books priced at $0.99 or more. We promise this will make sense in Chapter 6.)

But for most authors who have been featured, it's worth every penny. Most authors at least quadruple their money, and also have a 'sales tail' that can last for several weeks. It's also a great way to get reviews.

However, unfortunately, it's not easy to get accepted to BookBub. The Big 5 publishers use them frequently, so the competition is fierce. Some authors with incredible books, covers, and ratings have applied dozens of times without getting accepted.

So don't feel bad if you get rejected. Just keep working on your product quality and review quantity, and keep applying for new promotions every 6 weeks or so.

SITES THAT WILL PROMOTE YOUR BOOK FOR FREE

You might have heard there are sites out there that will list your book for free with no strings attached. Though the list is getting smaller, these places do exist.

The reason they offer this is because they are hoping to make sales through an affiliate program (normally Amazon Associates). So when someone clicks on their link to your book to purchase it, the promoter will receive a small percentage of money from the sale.

The problem with free sites is, you guessed it: you get what you pay for. Since they can list any book for free, the quality of books they offer might not be that great, so they may not have as many loyal subscribers. They also might only have one or two few free slots available in their newsletter, but they get requests for free promotions from everyone including Aunt Suzie, Tom Cruise, and your co-worker's sister's ex-husband from Mozambique.

Applying for these sites may be free, but it's also time-consuming unless you invest in an auto-submitter like the KDROI plugin for your internet browser (about $45). We think it's better to spend a little money on a promo site has a higher probability of working for your book rather than waste time on something that isn't likely to get good results.

If you still want to try your luck with free sites, here are a few that were free at the time of this book's publication (or have a free submission option). Make sure you read the guidelines carefully before submitting, and keep in mind, none of these sites guarantee a listing.

1. Armadillo Ebooks
2. E-reader Love
3. Deal Seeking Mom
4. Its Write Now
5. Pretty Hot
6. Freebies 4 Mom
7. YourNewBooks
8. Awesome Gang
9. Free99Books
10. I JustRead.It
11. BookGoodies
12. eFreeBooks

13. Free Discounted Books
14. Book Boost
15. BookHearts
16. Bookzio
17. eBook Lister
18. Mega Book Deals
19. Choosy Book Worm
20. Read Cheaply

PUT 'EM TO THE TEST!

Prepare to take some time to test out which websites return on their investment for you. It normally takes several months to a year to figure out which perform best for your book. There are a lot to test!

Here are some tips to discover the winners:

- **Test out one promo site every week.** Choose a day—Jamie started with Wednesday for some unknown reason—and offer your book for free or for a discount on that day every week for five weeks (using one free day per week should use up your five Kindle Free Days for each 90-day KDP Select enrollment period). Schedule a promotion with one different website on that same day within every consecutive week. This will give you clear data on how that single site performs for you on the day of the promotion, the day after, and five extra days for a 'sales tail.'
- **Pay attention to free downloads, ebook sales, Kindle Select/ Unlimited Pages Read, paperback sales, and audiobook sales.** Some promo sites might not generate a ton of ebook sales, but they might skyrocket your Pages Read. Some might generate a lot of traction for your audiobook version. And some might scoop up a staggering number of free downloads but not result in any sales. Try to calculate the true profit over time to determine an

accurate return on investment.

- **Look out for new reviews.** Reviews are like gold. Sometimes readers will mention where they got a copy of your book from in their review. Remember that reviews are priceless, as they increase your chances of being selected by a larger promo site like BookBub, and they increase the value of your book in buyers' eyes as they're collected over time.

- **Keep a detailed calendar record.** Track how websites perform over time, every time you use them. Some sites lose effectiveness over time, and some just keep getting better. You might also want to track your book's Amazon Best Sellers Rank.

- **Bribe a math nerd to make you a spreadsheet.** Yeah, spreadsheets give us headaches, too. But if you can get one to calculate your return on investment when you plop in numbers like the cost of the ad and the profit made, it'll be much easier over time to figure out which sites work the best for your book. Make sure to also note how many free downloads your promotion got, if it was a specific genre list within a promo site (ie, 'Robin Reads Thriller List' instead of just 'Robin Reads'), your Amazon Best Sellers Rank, and/or how many reviews you think resulted from that promo.

- **Don't use the same promotional website/newsletter list more than once every 6 months for the same book.** If you use the same promo site constantly, the effectiveness of your promotion will drop because you're advertising to the same audience over and over again. However, most promo sites continue to gather new subscribers, so a new ad every 6 months is still likely to catch some new eyes. Please note this doesn't include your own platform (your website, newsletter, and social media).

- **Don't stack promo sites on the same day until you've found what works for your book.** You might have heard the advice to 'stack' your promos—to schedule more than one promo site to feature your ad on the same day. And that's a great strategy ... *after* you've been doing this for awhile. When you start off, the most important thing is to collect data to figure out which sites work and which ones don't. Since most promo sites don't share their tracking data with you, and there's no way to determine how many free downloads, sales, or Pages Read came from which sites, it's better to try one at a time and keep track of your results. Remember—this is a marathon, not a sprint.

THE PROMO SITE SLEUTH

Besides checking with other authors on how a particular promo site does for your genre, there's another way you can get a rough idea of how your book might do. Since promotions generally start in the morning and take a bit of time during the day to generate sales, we suggest you do this check in the evening:

Go to the promo site you're interested in and find the book that's closest to your genre. Be as specific as possible (for instance, don't check a steamy romance if yours is squeaky clean). Click on the book's Amazon listing and scroll down to see where it's ranked. If it's in the top 10 of its Amazon category and in at least the top 5,000 in the Amazon store overall, then your book will probably do well on that promotional site.

If the book you're comparing is on a free promo, make sure you check the 'free' section in its category on Amazon. This book should be in the top 5 of its category and in the top 1,000 of Amazon's free books section. If this isn't the case, we don't suggest you try the site.

If Jamie and Angela had done this when they were just starting out, they would have saved hundreds, if not thousands, of dollars over time trying to figure out what worked for their books. We're just sayin'.

PROMO SITES TO AVOID

1. **Sites that promise ridiculous results.** Angela fell for a site that promised tens of thousands of downloads for her free book. She *did* get those downloads, but with that many she should have had at least dozens of sales of her other books. She had none. Turns out the site used bots to rack up sales, which is illegal per Amazon's TOS. Always check with other authors if something seems too good to be true. Please note: this is not the same as sites which give estimates of how many subscribers they have to a certain genre. These are just suggestions and not guarantees.

2. **Sites that promise positive reviews.** This was already covered but it bears repeating. Don't ever, *ever* pay for promised positive reviews. You could be kicked off Amazon in the blink of a fly's eye. (If a fly has eyelids. Not sure about that one.)

3. **Sites that promise movie contracts.** Yep, these exist. They will promise your book will be pitched to Hollywood producers for the low, low price of two thousand dollars. You can send your own books to Hollywood producers for a much cheaper price and probably have about the same chance of getting it turned into a movie.

4. **Sites that offer tons of extra stuff you don't need.** Book trailers on YouTube, press releases, etc ... Pay an expert graphic designer for that stuff if you want it down the road. It's not going to bring you sales right now.

5. **Contests.** This is a touchy subject because winning awards can look very good on your author resume. But many contests are scams, and even a good portion of the legitimate ones require a sizable reading fee. So when you're starting out, you might just enter contests that are free and see what happens. Before you spend a fortune on entry fees, see what your Amazon reviews say.

IT'S NOT WORKING AND I'M GOING TO CRY

If you have done what we suggested in *The Busy Mom's Guide to Writing* and invested in a good cover and editing, and your book is in a popular genre like romance, mystery, thriller, sci-fi or fantasy, you should at least be breaking even on inexpensive (under $25) promos at first. Especially if you're offering your book for free, because promotions for free books tend to cost less than promotions for discounted books.

If you're not at least breaking even with your paid promotions, there are a few reasons this could be happening:

1. The promo site you used might not be the best fit for your book
2. Your book might have been advertised next to a very similar book and overshadowed, like a bestseller in your genre or one with a more striking cover or more positive reviews
3. Some days and seasons, like certain holidays, don't generate as many book sales in general
4. Something crazy could have happened in the news and no one is thinking about recreational reading that day
5. It could just be a fluke… it happens

Don't give up on the first try. We have several great promo sites to recommend and one might work better than another.

If you are using our methods—which we and other indies have used time and time again—and you're not getting results, you might need to go back to the drawing board. You might have to take a good long look at your cover, blurb, and hooks in your first chapter (prospective buyers on Amazon can see a Kindle preview for free before purchasing), or you might need a fresh pair of eyes. Ask other authors to look at your cover and give you feedback on what they like and don't like.

Be willing to change and improve. If you want to make sales, you have to be willing to learn and adapt. With perseverance and humility, you'll get there—we promise.

Jamie and Angela have both learned this the hard (and expensive) way. But if we hadn't picked ourselves up and kept going, we would never have had the success we've experienced. If two hair-brained busy moms like us can do it, we know you can, too.

QUESTIONS:

1. How much do I want to budget for testing promotional websites for the first three months?
2. Which promo sites could be good fits for my genre?
3. How much time can I dedicate to marketing with paid promotions so I don't cut too deeply into my writing time?

Chapter 6

FREE PULSING:
OUR SECRET WEAPON

> "*Seek advice from the experts. You may think you know how to market your book, but unless you are trained in marketing, you are selling yourself—and your book— short.*"
>
> — Beth Wiseman, bestselling author of over 30 books and one of Jamie's clients

When we first started publishing books, neither one of us would have imagined giving our books away for free. After months of time and effort, would we really hand over pieces of our soul for nothing in return? It seemed ridiculous.

But then we began to consider how many books there were out there. Millions and millions of them. Narrow it down to our chosen genres, and there's still thousands. Like, hundreds of thousands.

Think about when you take your children to the library or bookstore. How many books do you have to choose from? Maybe you go in searching for a specific author. Perhaps your child wants a book about dinosaurs, or you are looking for a cookbook with crockpot recipes. Even if you're just browsing a section, you will still probably gravitate towards a certain subject or genre.

You might stumble upon a book that looks interesting by an author you've never read. But what if there are a hundred books in the genre you like on the shelves surrounding you? What if there are a thousand? What if there are *tens of thousands?*

Imagine your book is on that shelf. How likely is it to be noticed, even if it has a wonderful cover and a thrilling blurb on the back?

But consider this scenario. What if you walked into the bookstore with your children, and when you entered the children's section, a mysterious little man with a twinkling smile and a red hat came up to you and said, "Hello! You have a fine family there. Would your children like a book about chimpanzees?"

"Well, we were really looking for a book about dinosaurs," you say, "but thank you, my good man."

He hands you a brightly-colored paperback and says, "Oh, indeed. But you can have this book about chimpanzees... for *free.*"

Now, unless one of your children happened to be terrified of chimpanzees, you would probably take the book, right? You might buy a dinosaur book as well, but why not take the one about chimpanzees, since it's free?

And maybe one of your kids would read it on the way home, and decide chimpanzees were their favorite animals. And they might beg for every chimpanzee book written by that author. And every time a new book by that author came out, they might be first in line, waiting to buy it.

Now, we aren't in LaLa Land. Giving out a free book doesn't mean every time you'll find a reader for life who buys every single one of your books (or Angela's kids would be going to Disney World every week). But giving books away for free can be a great way to get exposure. Especially if no one has ever heard of you. (Great-Aunt Thelma in Ohio doesn't count, even if she buys your books for everyone in her bridge club.)

INTRODUCING FREE PULSING

Enter our favorite strategy—we've dubbed it 'free pulsing,' because it's similar to 'price pulsing,' a widely-used strategy where publishers occasionally drop the price on books to foster a resurgence of sales and ranking.

Free pulsing a book means offering it for free for *one day only*.

Please note: the free pulsing strategy can normally only be used for books in the KDP Select 90-day program. If your books are published on multiple ebook platforms, this method will probably not work.

Some people try this by changing the price of their ebooks to free on other providers (like Kobo) and then requesting Amazon price match. But this comes with risks. Amazon can take weeks to price-match something, and sometimes they refuse. And you will have to follow up and make sure everyone changes it back after the promo which could also take weeks. It renders the free pulsing method useless.

On your free day, schedule a paid 'free book' promotion with your favorite promotional website (see Chapter 5 to test out which promo sites work best for your book). Or if you're confident in the promotional sites and can get accepted for several promotions at once on the same day, it will boost your ranking even higher in a larger 'pulse.'

Normally this is done with the first book in a series, and it performs best for a complete series. Even though you're giving away your book for free that one day, you should make a profit in several different ways:

1. **Next day sales at full price.** Many people won't see the email from your promotional website until the next day, because let's face it—they were watching Texas A&M crush the Razorbacks and eating way too many cheese puffs. So they open up their email the next morning, see your promotion, think your book looks awesome, and happily pay full price for it.

2. **Kindle Select/Kindle Unlimited Pages Read.** Lots of voracious readers are in the Kindle Unlimited program, which we'll explain in the next section. For readers in this program, many accidentally click to 'borrow' the book through Kindle Unlimited instead of clicking to download it for free. When this happens, you get paid for their Pages Read.

3. **Sales on the next book(s) in the series.** If you have other books in the series available for sale, and you've written an awesome story with a great lead-in for the next book, you can expect a good sell-through rate and a 'sales tail' for the next several weeks as people devour your series.

4. **Sales on your future books.** There's always a chance that one of your new readers will love your books so much that they'll sign up for your email newsletter list and eagerly await the release of your next book. Heck, they might even join your beta reader team and become a priceless part of your future book launches (yes, this has happened to us more than once).

5. **Reviews: increasing future profits.** You will get new reviews when you give out free books. Don't expect an avalanche of them, but they will trickle in over time and steadily increase the chance that people who run across your book page will buy it in the future. We see about 1 review per 500 downloads.

KDP SELECT: ITS BARK IS BETTER THAN ITS BITE

In order to work with free pulsing for Amazon Kindle books, you will have to sign up for Kindle's KDP Select program. Joining Select enters your book into the Kindle Unlimited library on Amazon.com.

Kindle Unlimited is like Netflix for books. People pay Amazon a monthly subscription fee and get access to every book within the program at no additional charge. Amazon calculates how many pages of which books are read and pays authors accordingly, depending on how much money they made through subscriptions that month. (Pretty cool, right?) This extra income can be a huge boon to authors—even doubling our profits some months.

The catch is, when you opt to join KDP Select, you agree to only feature your ebook on Amazon Kindle for three months, as opposed to other ebook platforms like Nook, iBooks, and Kobo. Which sounds awful, and in many ways it is, but unfortunately the profits we make on these other platforms does not compare to how much we make from our Pages Read.

BEWARE THE KU WARZONE

Now, the KDP Select program (Kindle Unlimited) might or might not be your cup of tea. It's a controversial topic among authors. Everyone has an opinion, and their opinions tend to be strong. Like, launch-the-mortar-and-jump-in-the-foxhole strong.

But we recommend at least trying it out for one 90-day KDP Select enrollment period to see how it works for your books. You can always return your ebooks to other platforms (Nook, iBooks, Kobo, etc.) after your 90-day term is up.

However, it can be more difficult to remove ebooks from other platforms if you used a service like Smashwords or Draft2Digital, so be wary of that.

Another benefit you get with the Kindle Select program is the opportunity to schedule five days of promotions within every 90-day enrollment period. You can either have five Kindle Free Days, or five days of what is called a Kindle Countdown. You cannot use both, so choose wisely.

KINDLE FREE DAYS

Choosing Kindle Free Days lets you can schedule days where your book's Kindle version will be listed on Amazon.com for free. You get no compensation for books downloaded, but this also costs you nothing. You have five free days to use every 90-day Kindle Select enrollment period, but you do *not* have to schedule them all in a row (and we don't recommend it for the free pulsing strategy).

KINDLE COUNTDOWNS

If you don't want to use your book's free days, you can choose to schedule your book's price to reduce for five days in a row instead. So you can only schedule the Kindle Countdown to run once in the 90-day period, but you can change the price each day if you like.

For example, you could offer the book for $2.99 the first day, $1.99 the second day, and so on. Or you can offer it for $0.99 for each day.

The nice thing about this is you will get 70% of your $0.99 sales royalties for these days instead of the normal 35% at that price point. (Kindle royalties are normally at 35%, or 70% if the book is priced between $2.99 and $9.99.)

So what's not to like about Kindle Countdown deals?

Unfortunately, promoting with this method is becoming less and less effective. You can simply change the price point of your book to $0.99 whenever you like, anyway. And if you pay for promotions for a $0.99 deal, it's almost always a waste of your money.

In our experience—and those of our clients—you will almost always get better results in the long run with free pulsing.

"You busy moms are perpetuating free culture! Your horrible strategy is why publishers and bookstores are dying! It's abhorrent and frankly I'm appalled!"

Okay, okay. We don't like the modern 'I want everything for free' culture any more than you do. We like to be paid for our work, and we want you to be as well. It just so happens that free pulsing makes us more income than almost every other marketing strategy.

Free culture isn't just affecting the ebook market—it has become integrated into all other kinds of media including TV shows, video games, music, and art.

The most successful video games nowadays tend to be free-to-play, including most popular apps for your phone. YouTube and your grandpa's classic TV let you watch for free. The radio and apps like Pandora play free music. Netflix's subscription platform makes people feel like they're getting all the entertainment they want for free, and Kindle Unlimited works in the same manner for ebooks.

Why would you pay $5.99 for a Kindle ebook when there's a free book next to it that's just as appealing? You probably wouldn't give up your hard-earned cash unless you already knew that series or author—or had read a free sample and got hooked.

This is exactly what we're doing with free pulsing: offering a free sample of our writing so readers will gladly pay full price for the next book. And the next. And then buy the paperback version. And then tell their friends about it.

As soon as a better option arises, trust us, we'll take it. But for now, free pulsing is one of the most effective marketing strategies for giving our ebooks the most traction, visibility, and profit.

MAKING THE MOST OF YOUR KINDLE FREE DAYS

DON'T SCHEDULE FREE DAYS IN A ROW

Many authors and blogs will suggest that even though you don't have to, you should schedule all five of your Kindle Free Days in a row. They argue that this will keep the book elevated in the free section and the days will build on each other.

While this is true, we don't recommend this because as soon as your book isn't free anymore, it leaves the Free Books section and the benefit vanishes. Also:

1. **You'll lose most of your next day sales.** People may open their email the day after your sale and decide they want the book anyway, for the full price. If you have only one consecutive free period of five days, you will only experience this benefit once instead of five times from five separately-scheduled free days.
2. **Slow and steady wins the race.** Amazon's algorithms prefer books with steady sales over time, not huge spikes once every 90 days. This indicates to them that your book simply had a promotion, not necessarily that it's a great book that people keep wanting to buy consistently.
3. **Don't put all your eggs in one basket.** Something might happen around the time of your promotion—maybe a holiday, something scary in the news, or a random slump—that could make people less prone to book shopping during that time.
4. **I can't see!** If all of your paid promotions go off at the same time, you won't be able to tell how each one performed, and therefore which are the most profitable.

So we suggest that you schedule one free day at a time, perhaps one to two weeks apart. This requires some careful planning, but it's well

> ## We have seen great profit from next day sales
> time and time again. In fact, it's happening to Angela today.
>
> She promoted *The River Girl's Song* on a Kindle Free Day with a promo site called BookSends. The promo site cost $25. She had 433 free downloads on the day of the promotion. She also sold 9 copies of other books in the series for full price that day.
>
> The next day she sold 13 full-priced copies of *The River Girl's Song* along with 15 other books in the series. Not including Kindle Unlimited pages read, she made $74 on the ad, which is a $49 profit.
>
> Keep in mind this is just in two days—there's often a long 'tail' of sales after ads like this when readers finish the free book and buy the next one, sometimes weeks later.

worth it.

PLAN AHEAD CAREFULLY

If you are a forgetful person, or if you just have several small people demanding your time and brain cells like we do, then we suggest you get a desk calendar—or in Jamie's case, a giant calendar that takes up her entire wall—so you can keep track of promotions. We also recommend you set up a spreadsheet so you can keep track of promotion dates and sales.

Many of the really good promo sites require you schedule at least a few weeks ahead, and for some, calendars fill up a month or more beforehand. So make sure to schedule your promos early!

Try to avoid weekends and holidays. That way your book will be less likely to be lost in the millions. On the other hand, if you land a BookBub ad on a holiday, don't say no.

Also keep in mind that most sites limit how many times you can promote a specific book or author. For some it's once a month, for others it's every six months. This is another reason why it's important to keep writing new books, and why it's crucial you keep a record of where you advertise and when.

START OFF SLOW

Don't invest a ton of cash in your first batch of promos. Check your book budget carefully and set aside maybe $50 for the first month. Learn which promo sites work and which ones don't. Then you can invest with confidence. We like to see about 50 free downloads for every dollar we spend on an ad, though some places tend to do much, much better.

Remember, the most important goal at the beginning is to get your book out there to collect reviews, and to start building a fan base of readers. If you've broken even or made a profit within two days of your ad, you've had a good promo. Be patient—sometimes it takes 24 hours for Amazon to register free downloads and sales.

WHAT ABOUT STAND-ALONES AND LATER BOOKS IN A SERIES?

Some people like to wait until they have three or more books finished in a series before paying to promote them. That way readers can order them all at once, right off the bat, and the return on investment from promotions is higher.

This method is fine and works well, but we are way too impatient to wait for that. You can make money by free pulsing a stand-alone book or with only the first book in a series released, though not as much in the long run.

Yes, this sounds like madness. But we promise we have seen it work time and again, and it's a great way for new authors to build up rankings, sales, and most importantly, reviews.

If you have several books in a series, we recommend running free days on them all periodically and seeing what happens. This works very well if your books can be read separately from one another, and especially if your covers are very different. Sometimes different books in the same series can even do better because of their cover's subject matter.

For example, Angela's book two in the *Texas Women of Spirit* series, *The Comanche Girl's Prayer*, has a partially separate audience from *The River Girl's Song*. Its cover has a picture of a Native American girl with a horse, and some people specifically like reading books about Native Americans.

Try it out and see what happens, but as always keep records of how each book does with each promo site and method. You'll be glad you did.

SHOULD I FREE PULSE MY FULL SERIES BOX SET?

Giving away your full series for free can be terrifying, and we don't recommend you do it often. But our box sets have performed very well for us in both of our different genres.

When you find a promo site that performs very well for your books, most of the same rules of free pulsing apply—and the reasons you will profit. Except the full price of your series is probably much higher than your price for book 1, so your royalties from your next day sales should be even higher.

Several days ago, Jamie gave away the Kindle version of *The Sentinel Trilogy* box set for free for one day and promoted it with the website Book Barbarian. It was downloaded for free over 1,300 times. She spent $45 on the ad and made $154 in full price sales over the next three days. This doesn't include profit from thousands of KDP Select Pages Read, paperback sales, or the sales tail she's still enjoying. She's also expecting to see new reviews and purchases of a novella prequel to the series over the next few weeks.

This was Jamie's first time to free pulse one of her own full series, since the final book was just released a couple of months ago. Yes, it was scary, but she's so glad she tried it!

A CORD OF MANY STRANDS IS NOT EASILY BROKEN

At first, it may seem like these little bursts of sales aren't worth the investment of time and money. But when you spread your free pulsing days throughout the month, you will generally see steady sales, though smaller amounts—as well as Pages Read and profit through other avenues—throughout the month.

Here are several different ways we receive income:

1. **Steady Kindle ebook sales:** A few per day, thanks to continuous smaller marketing efforts
2. **Spikes of Kindle ebook sales:** Dozens at a time thanks to free pulsing promotions
3. **KDP Pages Read:** Both steady and spiking numbers with free pulsing. If you have 'gone wide' and not entered the KDP Select program, replace this line with ebooks sold on other platforms such as Nook, Kobo, and iBooks.
4. **Online paperback sales:** Both through Amazon.com and other retail bookstores such as Barnes & Noble
5. **Signed paperback sales:** Online sales of autographed copies that we sell through our websites or a bookstore we manage such as Gumroad
6. **Paperback sales at local stores:** This includes bookstores, local shops, and library sales
7. **Paperback sales at events:** Book signings, festivals, and meet-

and-greets that we attend and host a booth at

8. **Audiobook sales:** Generated through Amazon.com via the Audiobook Creation Exchange (ACX)

9. **Amazon Affiliates:** Earning back a percentage of sales through recommending our books and others with a special affiliate link

10. **Website ads:** Revenue generated from displaying ads on our website through services such as Google AdSense

Of course, everyone's sales experience will be different, but you can see how it all adds up. You really have to look at sales in terms of *months,* not *days,* and work on marketing on multiple fronts to achieve a steady income.

Now just imagine ... what could your income look like if you had another series out? What if your next series had five books in it instead of three? What could your career look like in five years if you market and write faithfully, treating it like your full-time job?

These thoughts get us pretty excited ... maybe even more excited than poolside margaritas in Cabo. Because, hey, maybe series number five could make those margaritas a reality.

QUESTIONS:

1. How do I feel about giving my book away for free? What are the pros and cons of giving it a try?

2. Could I write more books in my series to make my promotions more effective? What about my next series?

3. What method would be easiest for me to keep track of my free days and promotion results?

Chapter 7

PAY-PER-CLICK ADS

"Success is a journey, not a destination."

— Ben Sweetland

Ads. They interrupt our videos, flash weird images in our peripheral vision, and recommend awkward products just as someone else glances at our screen.

You hate them, and we hate them, too. Until they recommend the most adorable blouse, the perfect Father's Day gift, or those gluten-free cheese crisps that are simply divine.

Pay-per-click ads give you a way to advertise your books to millions of shoppers, and you only pay for the ad when people click on it.

This type of ad has a high learning curve. It can take a good amount of babysitting and refining, but when you discover which keywords and ad copy works for your books, boy, is it worth it.

AMAZON ADS

Amazon offers their own advertising program, AMS (Amazon Marketing Services). They have two differenttypes ads you can try:

1. **Sponsored Products:** Keyword targeted ads can display in search results and on product detail pages.
2. **Product Display Ads:** Product or interest targeted ads (for ebooks only) can display on product detail pages and Kindle eReaders.

For beginners, we suggest you go with Sponsored Product ads, which have performed best for us. The idea is to bid for slots below a popular Amazon product so that people who search for that product will also see your book.

Here's a quick guide on how to create a Sponsored Product ad:

1. **Go to the AMS website** at https://ams.amazon.com and select 'New Campaign.'
2. **Choose 'Sponsored Products.'**
3. **Select which book** you want to advertise.
4. **Campaign name:** Name your campaign whatever you want—the name is just for your records.
5. **Average daily budget:** Start with $1.00 for your cost per day. If the ad makes you dazzling sales right off the bat, you can adjust it whenever you like. At the end of the campaign, the average daily spend will not exceed your average daily budget.
6. **Duration:** Run your campaign for about 2 weeks. We run our ads for no longer than 1 month at a time. They tend to get kinda stale.
7. **Keywords:** Plan to add at least 200 keywords. Amazon will have suggested ones, but not all of them are great. We don't suggest using your author name or book title. Check below for our list of keyword suggestions.
8. **Cost-per-click (CPC) bid for suggested keywords:** Start with your CPC at 15 cents. You can always increase it later when a certain keyword performs better than others.
9. **Custom text:** Make your ad copy short and catchy. Use action

words like 'join,' 'experience,' 'read,' and 'ride along.' Amazon does not allow you to include claims like 'best selling' and you cannot use the word 'Kindle.' However, you *can* say free on Kindle Unlimited, and if your book is in the KDP Select program, we definitely recommend you use these words in your ad. Check out the section on writing ad copy later in this chapter.

10. **Hit the 'Submit campaign for review' button** and you're done!

It takes 12-24 hours for an ad to be approved. Amazon will notify you when it's up and running. Sweet!

TIPS FOR AWESOME AMAZON ADS

- **Experiment.** Copy your ad to use the same keywords and details, but try out different wording. Then see what performs the best! This can help you learn how to create better back cover copy for your books as well.

- **Pause when you hit your budget.** Set a monthly budget for your AMS ads. Once you've hit the budget, you can pause all the ads and try again the next month. We suggest starting with $20-$50 per month until you figure it all out. Expect to lose a bit of money the first month or so—this takes time and effort to find what works. But many authors say this is the best way to promote indie books out there.

- **Create a system for naming your ads.** Once you've started an ad, there is no way to remove it from your screen. You can 'pause' or 'terminate' an ad so it's not running anymore, but it will always be there, staring at you blankly from your dashboard. This makes your area get cluttered very quickly. So it helps to come up with a naming method to organize and quickly identify your ads. Jamie names all of her ads like this: "2018-05-Sentinel01-List3." This equates to: "(Year)-(Month)-(Book title)(Ad number for this book, which matches the ad copy in her notes)-(Keyword list)"

- **You can edit keywords, budget, and CPC bids** once an ad has been approved, but there is no way to edit the ad's wording. So you might think of one tiny little thing to change but you'll have to start all over again and make a new ad with the change. And—you guessed it—the old ad just stays there, even if it's terminated.
- **Reporting can be slow.** Sometimes sales take up to three days to be reported, *and* it doesn't report Kindle Unlimited Pages Read if you are in the Kindle Select program. Which is a real shame, because Jamie finds the most benefit from her AMS ads to be Pages Read. So we suggest running AMS ads by themselves with no other promotions at first, so you can get an idea of what sales they are bringing in.
- **Ads get stale.** We've found that AMS ads can go along great for a time, then start to stagnate and not work as well. Consider terminating those ads and creating new ones with the same or slightly different wording. You might even take a break for a week or two and start it up again. We don't know why it works that way. But it does.

FACEBOOK ADS

Some writers swear by Facebook ads, and they have been used as an effective form of marketing. But it's also an exact science that can take hours of time per day and, more importantly, hundreds of dollars before you figure out what will work.

Facebook has recently revamped their ads system and it has become even more complicated than before. Which is not to say the beast can't be tamed. They do have a very helpful system to teach users how to set them up.

We recommend you try running Amazon Marketing (AMS) ads before you try Facebook ads, and we'll get into the why later.

Here's a very brief rundown of how to set up a Facebook ad:

1. Go to the ads manager on your Facebook settings. You'll find it on your author page, under the rectangular cover picture, in the drop-down menu after 'like,' 'follow,' and 'share.' This will take you to a large graph-chart looking thing. You should see a green button that says 'create ad.'

2. Set a spending cap. This is great so you won't accidentally spend $1,000 (which can be done quickly, believe it or not). We recommend you start with a cap of $20 or so. You can always make it higher later.

3. Select a marketing objective. You can do all kinds of things with this, but we recommend choosing 'reach' from the 'awareness' column and 'engagement' from the 'consideration' column. You will see a round icon with two blue people on it. Choose the first button, 'post engagement' from the choices, then hit continue. Someday when you really want to go crazy you might want to try creating split tests and that sort of thing, but let's figure this one out first, shall we?

4. Create an audience. Pick the manual audience option. You can call this audience a name and save it, which you should do if you ever want to try another ad with the same audience in mind.

5. Choose your locations. We recommend countries that have the same native language as your book to start. For example, if your book is in English, you might choose the US, United Kingdom, Australia, and Canada for your audience (these are the countries we see the most ebook sales from overall). You can always check your Amazon Kindle sales to see which countries purchase the majority of your books if you are in doubt.

6. Select an age group. You might start off broad and then narrow it as much as possible as you collect data from your ads. For example, Angela targets women between the ages of 30 and 50 for her women's fiction books. You will probably have to do some testing to figure out exactly what age your book appeals to, but the great thing is Facebook will give you very specific charts of who clicks on your ads so you can tweak accordingly.

7. Choose your language in the same way you chose locations.

8. Detailed targeting. Okay, so here's where it gets tricky. You don't want to go with too broad of an audience here because you don't want to waste money on people who aren't really interested in your book. At the same time, you want the right people to actually click and buy. Here are a few tips on how to target your audience:

- **Go to Amazon and find the top ten authors in your genre.** Enter them in the detailed targeting space. If their names come up, add them to your targeting interest list. Note: Not all will come up, because not every author has a big enough presence on Facebook.
- **Type in your genre keywords to your best ability.** For example, 'romantic fiction,' 'steampunk,' or 'western books.' You may have to try several combinations before you find actual Facebook categories that will stick.
- **Think about your demographic.** Would your books be more interesting to college students? High school students? Stay-at-home moms? You can also use this to target specific careers and hobbies, which is especially helpful for non-fiction.

After you've entered a few of your own ideas, you can click the suggestions button. Add a few of these if you think they are relevant.

9. Set a budget. We suggest very strongly you set a low budget for a while until you get the hang of these ads, they can add up quickly. Start with maybe $2 per day, and remember you can turn it off at any time. With Facebook ads, you have no way to regulate how much it will cost per click—it all depends on the popularity of your topic and how many other advertisers are vying for the same audience. Under $0.50 per click is a good amount to hope for.

10. Schedule your ad. Start off with trying 1-3 days. You can always restart if your ad is doing spectacularly.

11. You can now choose to create an ad or use an existing post. We will go with creating an ad.

12. Choose your author page under Facebook page. Choose 'Single Image' under formatting.

13. Upload your image. We suggest a cropped picture of your cover with no text, or an image that has to do with your genre. Book covers themselves are not recommended because Facebook is picky about too much text in the ad's graphic. If you have no other options though, try your cover and see what happens. Angela cropped a portion of her cover with her MC's face and added a tagline, like this:

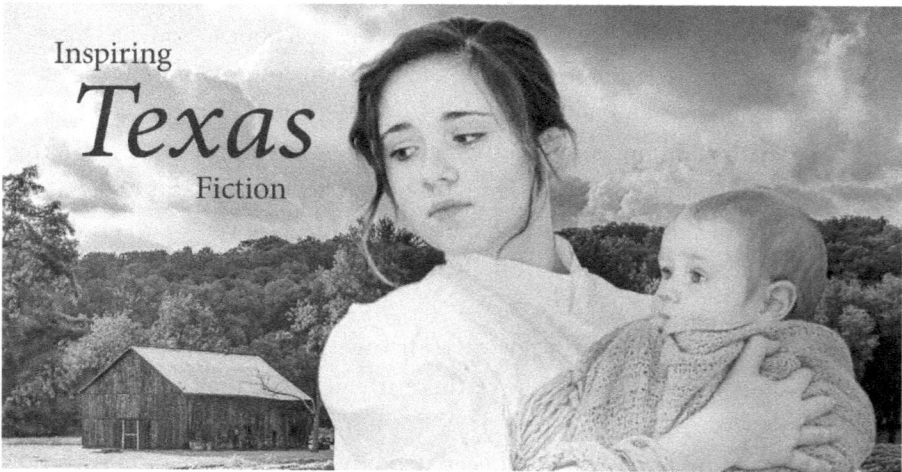

14. Write your ad. Use short, catchy lines that catch people's attention. Consider trying action words that involve the reader like 'join,' 'experience,' 'try,' 'enjoy,' and 'catch.' Don't forget to include a link to your book!

15. Submit your ad to Facebook and wait for it to be approved. This may take a few tries before you get it right, so don't give up.

PROS AND CONS OF FACEBOOK ADS

As of this publication, there is no way to know exactly how many sales you make with Facebook ads; you can only see how many clicks you get. This is why we suggest you run your Facebook ads alone, while no other promotions are going on, to give you a better idea of how well they are working.

Even though this is a con when compared to Amazon ads, there's one benefit unique to Facebook ads. When you go to notifications on your Facebook page and see that people have clicked 'like' on your ad, you will also have the chance to invite them to 'like' your Facebook page. This is a great way to get more Facebook fans, which is in turn rewarded by Facebook, since the more likes you get the more visible your posts will be.

We recommend reading other craft books that specialize on teaching you Facebook ad strategies before jumping in face-first. It can be massive waste of money if you're not careful.

BOOKBUB ADS

BookBub ads seem awesome because, well, it's BookBub, right? One would naturally assume since BookBub featured deals are so great, a BookBub pay-per-click ad could be very good, too.

Well… kinda.

BookBub ads are similar to Facebook ads. You bid on how much you are willing to pay for people to click on your ad and give a limit to how much you are willing to spend over all.

If you decide to try BookBub ads, we recommend you start with AMS ads or Facebook ads to figure out what keywords and ad copy works for your book. We also suggest you start with a small amount to spend over all (like $25) to see if you generate any sales. This money could vanish like lightning.

In our experience, we have not done amazingly well with BookBub ads considering how much we've spent. But we're not experts on it, and it might work great for you and your books. So it's up to you if you want to give it a try. As long as you've got a solid budget, it can't hurt to get your toes wet.

GOOGLE ADWORDS

The Google search engine is a gigantic platform used by millions of people every day, and using Google Adwords can be effective marketing for some authors.

As with BookBub ads, we suggest you spend some time working with Facebook and AMS ads before you delve into Google Adwords to learn what keywords and ad copy work for you. Google Adwords are not necessarily a good choice for book marketing because it's such a large playing field and it's harder to pinpoint a target audience.

But if you want to try it, we suggest starting out with a small amount and building up with more once you see success.

IDEAS FOR GATHERING KEYWORDS

Finding hundreds of keywords may seem daunting at first, but they add up fast. You will need a rolling few hundred keywords to keep your ads fresh. Try to start out with at least a hundred.

The best way to come up with keywords is to think, *If someone was searching for my book, what would they type in to find it?* Is it a space opera? Does it have vampires? Or a bromance? What about politics or religion? Does a dragon make an appearance? Does it take place in a specific historical time period? Or the apocalypse?

Below are our top suggestions for finding awesome keywords. Or, if you have more money than time, you can pay for a tool called KDP Rocket. It's a bit pricey, but it will save you hours of time by generating keywords for you. If AMS ads work well for you, this might be a good investment.

1. Type your genre in the search bar in Amazon and add everything that comes up as a suggested term. For example, if you've written a science fiction novel, you will see things like 'science fiction books,' 'science fiction ebooks,' 'science fiction bestsellers,' etc. Remember, this doesn't have to be what your book is, just what you want your book advertised with.
2. Brainstorm movies and TV shows similar to your book's genre
3. Grab the top twenty book titles in your book's genre
4. Authors in your book's 'also bought' list.
5. The last names of popular authors in your genre, even if they are common. ('Miller,' 'Johnson,' etc.)

IDEAS FOR WRITING AD COPY

Some sites will create their own verbiage for your book ad. After all, they've been promoting books a long time and they know what their readers want.

But for most sites, you can copy and paste parts of your book's blurb (back cover copy) and that will work fine. Be sure to add an eye-catching tagline.

For example:

- From best-selling/award-winning author … (if this is true, of course)
- 5-star review from (editorial reviewer or journalist)
- Over 100 five-star reviews!
- Sizzling romantic read

- Juicy drama you won't be able to put down
- The perfect beach read!
- Teaches children about …
- Cozy snuggle-up-by-the-fire mystery
- The classic whodunnit with a romantic twist
- Bone-chilling horror that'll make you sleep with a nightlight for a week
- Clean, sweet fiction for every heart
- Thrilling summer reading

Be creative and look at other book ads for ideas. Keep records to determine which copy works best for your book over time. Then when the numbers declare which copy performs best, you can learn how to write better ad copy over time—and write more compelling text for the back covers of your books. Cool beans!

QUESTIONS:

1. Do I want to invest in Kindle Rocket or spend the time finding keywords for myself?
2. How much money do I want to set aside for pay-per-click ads monthly until I figure out if they work for me?
3. What are some good one-sentence taglines I could use in my ads?

Chapter 8

MAGICAL UNICORN
GIVEAWAYS

"For the multifold secret to work only one thing is necessary. You must take action. You must give. You must share... Send out waves of love and kindness into the world and then simply wait for the response."

— John Kremer

We already told you to give your book away for free. Now what could we possibly ask you to give away in addition to that?

Don't worry—it's not your book this time.

Prize-oriented giveaways are a great way to get people interested in your books, or at least to sign up for your email newsletter list. If you give away something tempting that's not your books themselves—such as an Amazon gift card—people might buy your book in addition to signing up for the giveaway. If you give away your book as the prize, people who might have bought the book could instead think, "Maybe I'll win it!" and move along.

Giveaways are great for attracting people to your book signing booth at events, for cross-promoting with other authors in your genre, and for getting hundreds of people to sign up for your email newsletter list. Here are our favorite methods that we do regularly!

CREATING YOUR OWN GIVEAWAY

Before you set up a giveaway, you need to decide a few things:

1. **What is the objective of your contest?** Do you want Facebook followers? Newsletter subscribers? Twitter followers? Many giveaway platforms let you list a dozen or more ways for people to enter, but we recommend you only use 3-5. Put the most important one first. We suggest focusing on newsletter subscribers.

2. **What do you want to give away?** Remember, you're footing the bill for this. However, the better the prize, the more likely people are to do the tasks to enter the contest more times. We suggest a prize with a value between $25 and $50.

3. **How many items do you want to give away?** We suggest 1-5 prizes.

4. **How will you promote your giveaway?** We think the best way is to get other authors in your genre involved. Ask if they want to split the cost of the prize with you while you as the host handle the creation of the giveaway, shipping of the prize, and distribution of email addresses from the entries later. Then have each author promote the giveaway to their audience. Multi-author giveaways are mutually beneficial, so most of the time people you invite will accept!

OUR GO-TO PRIZE IDEAS

- **Gift card:** Amazon.com always works great but if you're hosting a physical event, try a gift card from a local restaurant.
- **Other books:** A book or set of books by a popular author in your genre. We don't recommend giving away your own book, so people won't be discouraged from buying it.
- **Genre-related goodies:** A hand-crafted item fans of your genre will enjoy from a site such as Etsy, like a stuffed dragon. a piece of Steampunk jewelry, a handmade bookmark, or a quill pen.
- **Swag from your brand:** A piece of art such as your book cover, an illustration from your book, or a map from your book in poster form. You can slap these things on a mug, T-shirt, stress ball—you wouldn't believe how many options are out there. Check out Zazzle.com for inexpensive ideas for easily-produced, high-quality swag.

RAFFLECOPTER

There are a lot of giveaway hosting services out there, but we prefer Rafflecopter. They offer a very simple way to hold a contest, and are especially helpful if you want to offer something besides books (like a gift card). In fact, if you only have one book, we suggest you give away something else, because the whole point is to get people interested in buying your book. If they think they're going to win it, they might not be as likely to buy it.

You can use the Rafflecopter service for free but we highly recommend you splurge on the $13 a month service, which allows you to add a picture of your prize (which can be super important) and design your own entry form. You can cancel it after one month if you don't want to do another contest for awhile.

To create your Rafflecopter giveaway, first design a graphic with a photo of what you are giving away and a description, because Rafflecopter doesn't give you much space to describe the prize. But keep text on the graphic itself to a minimum.

Decide on your terms and conditions. Will it be open to US residents (or your country) only? International shipping of any physical items can get very pricey. Will it be open to ages 18 and up or younger? This can get into some legal complications, so we tend to only allow people 18+ to enter.

Rafflecopter has a very easy-to-follow tutorial. Once you have built your contest, you can then embed it on your Facebook page. Rafflecopter will give you a link to share and also an HTML widget to use for your website, blog, etc.

Share your Rafflecopter with as many people as possible. Trade mentions with other authors on blogs, newsletters, retweets, etc.

PROMOTE YOUR GIVEAWAY

Submit your Rafflecopter to contest and giveaway websites to get the maximum reach. Some of the sites are free, while others charge $5 or more for the exposure. Here are a few of the sites we've used:

- Giveaway Frenzy: https://giveawayfrenzy.com
- Online Sweepstakes: http://www.online-sweepstakes.com
- Giveaway Promote: https://www.giveawaypromote.com
- Blog Giveaway Directory: https://www.bloggiveawaydirectory.com
- Sweetie's Sweeps: http://sweetiessweeps.com
- Win A Sweepstakes: http://winasweepstakes.com

AMAZON GIVEAWAYS

Amazon has a little-known, free way to get people to follow you on your Amazon author page—all you pay for is the prize.

You can set up an Amazon giveaway for your Kindle books (and, actually, you can give away anything on Amazon.com while you're at it.) Just go to the bottom of the product page and click to offer that item as a giveaway. (Note: this only works in the United States).

The coolest aspect of Amazon giveaways is the ability to make it public, meaning that it'll be listed in the Giveaway section of Amazon.com. This page gets so many visits that if you set up your giveaway with high odds for entrants to win, your giveaway could be completed and your prizes distributed within hours.

You can choose to give away one or multiple Kindle books—we suggest going with five. When the contest asks you how people can enter, you will have several options including getting them to follow you on Twitter, tweeting a message, and following your author page. We recommend you select the 'Follow on Amazon' option, especially if you are going to be marketing more than one book, because Amazon sends out email alerts to your followers every time you release a new book.

You will be able to choose which way a winner will be selected. We suggest you select the sweepstakes option where the winners are chosen at the end (Angela's preference), or the Random Instant Winner option where people have a chance to win a prize instantly (Jamie's preference). Run your contest for 3-7 days.

And make sure you check the box to make the giveaway public—this is crucial! If you don't do this, you will be the only one who knows about your giveaway. The crickets will sing you a lonely chorus.

When your giveaway goes live (normally it takes less than an hour), Amazon will send you a link you can use to monitor your contest and see how many people will enter. At the end of the contest, the number of entries you have will be the number of new Amazon followers you have. Yahoo!

The only frustrating thing about this is that as of now, there is no way to know how many Amazon followers you have. Why? It's a mystery only the Great and Powerful 'Zon knows.

Regardless, public Amazon giveaways are a good way to gain exposure and build your Amazon followers to be notified about your next book release.

NOTE: Between the writing process and formatting for this book, we heard that Amazon began phasing out their giveaways, or at least some mysterious part of it. It now only works for some people, some books, and some formats—we can't see any rhyme or reason to it at the moment. Imagine us screaming like Luke Skywalker: "Nooooooooo!" Sorry this note is so vague, but hopefully you can still give it a try and see if it will work for you. In the meantime, we'll have our fingers crossed for Amazon to smooth everything out and get their giveaways up and running again.

GOODREADS GIVEAWAYS

Goodreads used to be a free, easy way to give away a paperback and generate a few reviews. Jamie used to host one every month and would get around 600-1,200 entries every time. It was free to enter and free publicity—all the author had to pay for was the cost of the paperback prize and the shipping to get it to the winner. Jamie would also include a hand-written note of congratulations and a humble request for the winner's honest thoughts of the book in a review. Maybe every third or fifth winner would actually leave a review.

Well, apparently all good things must come to an end, because now Goodreads charges $119-$599 to list giveaways with them. Without really offering anything new.

What a gut punch.

This caused a massive uproar in the author community, as you can imagine. The vast, vast majority of authors no longer list giveaways with Goodreads, and will be reviling them for years to come. How this Amazon-owned company thinks six hundred dollars is worth maybe a couple of reviews, we'll never know.

JOINING AN EXISTING MULTI-AUTHOR GIVEAWAY

A great way to work with other authors is to join multi-author giveaways with services like BookSweeps. It costs about $60 for you to join the giveaway, but it normally results in hundreds of new subscribers for your email newsletter. Potential buyers! Yay!

With BookSweeps—Jamie's favorite—you can sign up for their newsletter to be notified when new giveaways become available. They tend to host genre-specific giveaways for one week at a time, but they are planned months in advance.

Dozens of authors with books similar to yours agree to give away two copies each: one for the grand prize winner and one for the runner-up. BookSweeps buys a shiny new e-reader like a Kindle Fire or Nook to give away with the grand prize.

BookSweeps creates promotional material like graphics and marketing copy for you to share with your social media followers and existing newsletter subscribers, encouraging them to sign up for the giveaway. When the dozens of other authors in the giveaway do this as well, the giveaway entries become a pool of people interested in your genre. At the end of the contest, BookSweeps will send you a spreadsheet with all of their emails for you to add to your newsletter list.

So all the authors have to do is pay the entry fee and share the contest with their followers, and entrants get to discover new authors in their genre. Win-win!

WELL, NOW I'VE GOT ALL OF THESE NEW EMAIL SUBSCRIBERS... WHAT DO I DO WITH THEM?

Jamie likes to send new subscribers to her newsletter a personalized email welcoming them to her list. She reminds them how they became subscribed through the giveaway and introduces herself and her books. She tells them that her newsletter will offer them other giveaways, updates, and goodies every month.

She also gives them a free digital copy of the book they would have won in the contest, anyway. This way they can have a free sample of her writing to know whether or not they'd want to stay subscribed to her list, and who knows? Maybe they'll like it and buy the other books in the series.

PERMANENT GIVEAWAYS: ENCOURAGING NEWSLETTER SIGN-UPS ON YOUR WEBSITE

If you are writing or promoting a series, we seriously recommend you have a short story or some other little digital freebie to give people when they sign up for your newsletter on your website. This will get you far more sign-ups over time than not offering anything.

Maybe a short spin-off story based on characters in your book, or a short prequel. Some people put together a collection of recipes, poems, and other fun articles based on characters in their series, while other authors offer free printable downloads of maps or bookmarks. Be creative!

SET UP AUTORESPONDERS

Most email services including MailChimp and MailerLite offer the ability to make a 'welcome to my newsletter' email that automatically is sent when someone signs up. In this email, make sure you include information about the freebie and where they can download it.

It's also a great idea to set up automatic emails to send new subscribers a week or two later, asking them how they liked the book, requesting an honest review, and offering a discount on the next book in the series.

BUT HOW DO PEOPLE DOWNLOAD THEIR FREE EBOOKS?

You have a few options here. One is to set up a 'hidden' page on your website with the MOBI, EPUB, and PDF files for people to download. The only way people can have access to these files is by getting the magic link after they've subscribed.

Another way to do this is by signing up with a place like Instafreebie or Book Funnel. Both of these services make it easy for people to get your book downloaded in their preferred format, and they handle questions about how people can get the files onto their ereader device.

Book Funnel has a plan that starts at $20 a year, but this plan does not include email integration. Instafreebie starts off as free, but costs $20 per month if you wish to include email integration. We always suggest starting off with the least expensive method and working your way up, or learning how to do it yourself.

QUESTIONS:

1. What could I offer as a permanent giveaway for people who sign up for my newsletter?
2. Do I want to plan a Rafflecopter giveaway? What would I offer as a prize? What other authors in my genre could I ask to join my giveaway?
3. Would it be worth it to sign up for a BookSweeps giveaway to build my newsletter audience?

Chapter 9

SIGNINGS, BOOTHS,
& EVENTS

"I've said it before, and by gosh, I'll say it again—don't be afraid to toot your own horn."

— Emlyn Chand

In your author dreams, chances are you've had that vision of being in a major-name bookstore, sitting at a table piled with your books, with a line of people out the door eagerly waiting for your signature across the creamy page.

Let's be honest. You probably have pages in your high school notebooks where you practiced your autograph just in case. Right? Okay, maybe we're the only ones.

Of course, as a mom, your deepest dream could be an entire half hour in the tub without being interrupted. But we digress.

Book signings can be great ways to meet people locally and drum up interest in your stories. They can also be a dismal way to spend a rainy, lonely afternoon (and yes, we have been there). So here are some suggestions for having the best book signings possible.

THROWING A LAUNCH PARTY OR BOOK SIGNING

A book launch party can be very profitable and a great way to introduce your book to the community. Friends and family will (hopefully) be excited that you've started this brave new journey, and they will probably come out to get an autographed copy of your paperback baby. Speaking of children, please get a sitter for these things. Unless you have an older child who likes to help haul heavy boxes of books.

We only recommend doing one of these—for your first book. The only exception to this would be if you have built up a huge local fan base of readers that will be sure to come.

1. Find a place to host your event. A local bookstore might work, if they have a reasonable space for you to put your table (and are open to indie books if yours are self-published). But you may have to pay a percentage of all items you sell, and if you have a bunch of family members and friends coming to buy your books, you might not want to

Even if you decide not to do a launch party or book signing right away, you might still want to order a few paperbacks to have on hand. Make one post on your Facebook page (only one—don't spam!) to see if anyone wants you to order a copy. You might be surprised how many you sell.

On the other hand, don't get your feelings hurt if you don't get a lot of interest. Some people just aren't interested in stories about magical samurai zombie-slaying princesses. And that's okay. Plenty of other people will be.

give up all that money.

Check around. A coffee shop, bakery or small cafe might have a space they don't mind you setting up in for a few hours, especially if it means bringing in a few hungry customers.

2. Promote. Send out personal invitations to folks with Amazon links so they can check out your book (and order online if they can't make it!). We recommend using your email newsletter, Twitter, and Facebook to spread the news, but you might also consider postcards for relatives who aren't tech-savvy but still like to read.

3. Ask people to let you know how many books they want. This way you'll have a basic idea of how many you need to order before the event. Please *don't* order 100 extra books and hope they will sell. They'll probably end up sitting in your garage and will be super heavy to haul around. If you have to, you can always take orders when you run out.

4. Bring an assistant. Okay, this isn't absolutely vital, but it's helpful to have someone there to run to the store for things you forgot, help with refreshments, and set up/tear down. And it's nice to have a buddy to chat with if the event ends up not being as rambunctious as you'd hoped.

5. Plan for a 2-3 hour time period. Any longer than that, and you might end up spending a long evening alone. It's also best to have your event in an evening or on a weekend, when fewer people will be at work or school.

6. Attract attendees with free goodies. If you're having your book signing in a public place like a bookstore or coffee shop, consider bringing a 'draw' item, like an inexpensive door prize, giveaway, cookies, or bookmarks. Think of something that relates to your target audience.

For example, if you have a children's book, consider handing out coloring sheets and a few crayons. Candy or chocolate is usually a universal hit. Make sure everything you hand out has your name and website attached to it somehow.

Don't invest a ton of money in swag right away. Keep your costs down until you've had a few signings under your belt.

FINDING LOCAL PLACES TO SELL YOUR BOOKS

This seems like a no-brainer, right? The place most people would think about selling books would be a bookstore. But you can find readers almost anywhere. And what happens when you're in a bookstore? You're surrounded by competition.

So while we recommend finding indie-friendly bookstores to work with (see Chapter 10), you might not see your best results at bookstore events. Angela sells more paperback books at craft booths during the holidays than anywhere else. Some writers sell well at comic-con type convention center places. Think outside the box.

1. Local markets. Many towns have farmer's markets or flea markets that meet every week which are open to locally-produced goods. Check with them to see how they feel about books. These are especially great for books written about a local region or DIY nonfiction, but authors of other genres can find success in these places as well.

2. Genre-specific events. Religious fiction might do well at church gatherings and events. Children's picture books might do well at carnival fundraisers and holiday fun events (like fall festivals and ice cream socials). Sci-fi and fantasy books do well at Jamie's favorite nerdy conventions. Hey, sometimes a purple alien costume sells more books... Ahem.

3. Craft booths. We recommend you aim for indoor, larger shows that attract a good number of shoppers. Well, you can do outdoor events if you want, but after we did an all-day Fourth of July booth in the Texas heat, we were kind of turned off to them. (Heavens have mercy.)

Most small towns have community craft bazaars, and many churches and private schools also host these events. We recommend you start looking for these booths several months in advance, since they fill up quickly. Try to find other vendors who've had booths at the same events in the past to find out if they had good sales.

We also recommend starting small; don't spend hundreds of dollars on ten events before you've had a chance to get your toes wet and find out what works.

4. Friends of the Library events. Many town libraries have Friends of the Library clubs. Find out who heads up group events and see if they would be open to you giving an author talk. If your book is a children's book, see if you can do a reading and bring copies to sell.

Note: some libraries will not allow you to sell your book at events. However, they might be open to you handing out bookmarks or business cards. It's a great way to get exposure.

5. Comic shops and gaming stores. If you write sci-fi or fantasy, you will most likely find kindred spirits in a comic shop. You might also try video game stores, card shops (like Magic or Pokemon), or tabletop gaming venues (Dungeons & Dragons, Warhammer, etc).

6. Gift shops and consignment stores can be good places to sell books or cookbooks. Consignment sales are possible in shops that rent shelves or booths to artists for a monthly fee or a percentage of sales.

QUESTIONS TO ASK BEFORE AN EVENT

1. What products does the event allow to be sold? (Some craft shows only allow hand-crafted items or baked goods.)

2. Do you provide tables and chairs, or do we need to bring all our own displays?

3. When should we come to set up? At what time do we need to be packed up and out?

4. How many customers do you generally see in a day?

5. How do you promote this event? Can I get a graphic to share for my social media?

6. How much space is available per booth?

7. Are power outlets accessible at the booth location?

8. Do you have free WiFi and/or good phone reception? (At one event out in the boonies, we ended up having to trek people to the railroad tracks across the street because our phones weren't connecting to our credit card processing programs. Fortunately, it was a small town with a bunch of patient people!)

9. Do we need to have a tax number ID form with us? (Every state is different, so check your state's sales tax requirements.)

WHAT TO BRING TO EVENTS

Here's our checklist of stuff to bring to events. They're not all necessary, but they sure are helpful!

1. Table and chair(s), if the event does not provide them. If you have more than a few books to promote, you might want to have two tables: one for books and one for your promotional materials, door prize, etc.

2. Books to sell! We don't recommend you sell the farm to purchase books for an event until you get some idea how well they will sell. 10-15 of each title should be sufficient. If you're also selling swag on the side like bookmarks or crafts, be sure to pack those, too.

3. A permanent or pen to sign your books with. Yes, people will ask for autographs. Yes, you will get a thrill. Jamie is super OCD about having a clickable permanent marker on hand to sign books with. They don't tend to run out of ink, and the signature looks all special and satisfying.

4. Signage or banners. What size and type of signage you can display will depend on the event. If you want to focus on a giveaway prize, you can attach a small banner to the table or hang it from the wall behind you. We like to take laminated pictures of our full book covers. (Staples has great deals on full-color prints if you request premium paper and not photo paper). They are eye-catching and very affordable.

Check out your local print shop for fast service and good prices. Or Vistaprint and UPrinting are great places to order inexpensive banners and signage online. They also have great deals on business cards and promotional postcards. Try to keep your printed materials generic (avoiding dates and event names) so you can re-use them at future events and keep your costs low.

5. Easy-up. If you are doing an outdoor event, an easy-up is a *must* unless you enjoy being sunburned. Most outdoor events require you bring weights for any easy-up or tent. We also recommend some kind of sides that can roll down in case of rain.

For your first event, you might consider borrowing or renting a tent to see if the cost will be worth it for long term. Of course, easy-ups are handy for many other occasions, like holiday gatherings and beach trips.

6. Displays to show off your books. With any product display, it's nice to have different levels to make the best use of your space. You don't have to spend a ton of money, though. Jamie uses a TV stand she found online for only $25 that's very easy to set up and take down. Angela likes to wrap a few cardboard boxes in seasonal wrapping paper or use wooden crates to prop up books. Bring props that go with your genre, such as a cowboy hat or magnifying glass. Be creative!

7. Tablecloth. Doesn't have to be fancy—a clean sheet will do in a pinch.

8. Drinks and snacks for the day, unless you want to spend all your profits on food.

9. Scissors, tape, and pens.

10. Bookmarks or business cards with your name, website or Amazon page, and contact email. It's also great to have your book cover on the back of your business card so it's easy for people to remember and look up when they get home. Some people prefer ebooks or don't have cash on hand to buy your paperback. When designing a business card, keep it simple. A picture of you or your logo, your name, e-mail, website, and your Amazon page address should be plenty of information.

11. Book stands. You will want several of these, because you're going to keep writing more books in the future, right? You can pick these up cheap from Amazon or a craft store like Hobby Lobby. Cheap plate stands can double well as book stands. Just don't take your grandma's.

12. A small door prize, such as an Amazon gift card. We don't recommend including books in these, since you don't want people to decide not to buy your book in the hopes they'll win it. This prize will be used to collect email addresses for your newsletter, and as a draw to your booth. We suggest adding a few larger items to make it eye-catching, like coffee gift sets, candy, or some other little gifts. It does not have to be expensive—we keep ours under $20.

13. A way to collect email addresses. This could be a clipboard, little slips of paper, or tickets for people to write their email addresses on as entry slips to your giveaway. It's also a way for you to contact them if they win. Make sure you clearly state that the addresses will be added to your email newsletter list. Grab a pack of cheap pens and a bowl to keep entry slips in.

14. Bags for placing purchased merchandise in. Sometimes people have a lot to carry, and they'll really appreciate it!

15. Cash for change and a way to process credit cards. Angela uses a Square card reader, and Jamie uses a PayPal-connected swiper. They connect to the headphone jack in their phones but can be used with tablets as well. Both are free, and charge a very small percentage of the sales you make through their service. Probably 50% of sales at any given event come from credit cards, at least in our experience. Grab and test a card reader beforehand, because you'd hate to miss out on sales from the people who forgot to bring cash!

16. Notepad, planner, or daytimer. You never know when someone might tell you about another show or event, or some other nifty info that might be forgotten.

17. Proof of Sales Tax ID. This will vary from state to state, so find out your local sales tax ID information. Some booth organizers require that you have a paper with your ID number or some kind of certification with you at all times, just in case the IRS comes looking around. We have never been asked for this information by an IRS agent, but you never know and we suppose it's better to be safe than sorry.

Keep in mind that anything you bring for an event has to be hauled in and set up, and then torn down and loaded again. Try to find lightweight, uncomplicated displays and shelving. Bring a dolly if you have one. You'll thank yourself at the end of the day.

TIPS TO MAKE THE MOST OUT OF YOUR EVENTS

- **Share with other authors.** Find authors in your area who like to do local events and see if you can share booth fees/duties. This is especially helpful for events that span over several days or have more expensive booth fees. Jamie and Angela met at a book signing event several years ago. They've done dozens of events together and haven't strangled each other yet.

- **Aim for indoors.** We aren't saying to never do outdoor booths, but if indoor is an option, choose it. The last thing you want to do is lose books to rain or have to chase your posters down the street. And if it's winter in Minnesota or summer in Texas, well … you get the drift.
- **Be outgoing and friendly.** If you hide behind your booth, you'll have much less interaction with passerby and therefore less sales. Believe in your book and be excited about it, and other people will be as well. But don't go overboard. No one likes to listen to a 30-minute sales pitch. Be genuine and put the needs of others before your sales quota. If you make a personal connection, people will buy your book just because they like you.
- **Keep your expectations low.** Some events are smashing successes, and some are not. If you have a less than successful book signing, don't think that it's because your book is terrible. Jamie and Angela have both had their share of negligible book events. It happens. We are so sorry, and we send you virtual hugs.

EVEN IF YOU DON'T MAKE A TON OF SALES…

- It's awesome to see firsthand reactions to your covers and blurbs. The questions people ask can be extremely helpful in gauging your audience.
- Make sure people know your books are available on Kindle. We've had people order every book we'd written right there on their phone while standing at our booth.
- Send your business card with everyone who shows interest. They might save up for it and buy your book with their next paycheck. If it's close to Christmas or their birthday, they might use a gift card to buy your book. Or they might pass the card along to someone else they think might enjoy your genre.

- Networking with event coordinators, other authors, and passerby can be invaluable. Angela landed another gig from a fellow author at one event, then ended up doing two new events that she made hundreds of dollars from. Always treat everyone as a future reader.

QUESTIONS:

1. What are three possible venues I could contact about hosting a book signing?
2. Should I plan a local launch party? Do I have enough local friends and family to make it worthwhile? Is there a local author friend I could ask to join me?
3. How much do I want to budget for my next event? (Calculate how many books you want to bring, and how much it will cost to order from your printer. Add it to any supplies you need, and consider making plans to save up for new equipment that might make future events easier.)

Chapter 10

BOOKSTORES,
LOCAL SHOPS, LIBRARIES, & SCHOOLS

"Don't give up before you get off your feet. Put the time in to learn what you can, build relationships, and develop quality content."

— Heather Hart

We covered book signings in Chapter 9, but selling at one event for one day is completely different than establishing a long-term relationship with a business owner. If you can get your foot in the door, a lasting relationship with a business owner can be a wonderful thing for both of you.

Your obvious first stop would be a locally-owned bookstore. We aren't saying not to try the big chain stores, but you might want to call the national office or check online for information before approaching a local manager. Many chain stores have policies in place which prevent them from featuring local authors without solicitation, which means they have contracts with book publishers and will not usually feature indie books in their stores. On the other hand, certain chains love to support local authors and often have a shelf set aside just for us. So always check.

If you are going to approach the owner of a local store, call ahead of time to find out the best day to come by. Here's some conversation starters you can draw from if you need ideas:

1. "Hello, I'm a local author. Could I please speak to your manager or owner?" (This will establish that you aren't trying to sell them ink or toner or something).
2. "Hi, my name is (your name) and I'm a writer. Do you feature books from local authors in your store?"
3. "Hey there! I saw your display on books from local authors, and I have a new release your customers might be interested in. Is there a good time I could come by for a few minutes and meet with you?"

Make sure you have a calendar in front of you and a notebook. Listen carefully. The store owner might not allow indie books on the shelves,

---

Use the words 'local author' instead of 'indie author.' Some bookstore owners have a stigma against indies, because, unfortunately, many indie books are badly produced and riddled with mistakes. But of course your book is awesome, because you took all of our advice from *The Busy Mom's Guide to Writing* and *The Busy Mom's Guide to Indie Publishing*, and you have an amazing cover and a carefully edited manuscript.

We're not saying to lie to the owner. Just don't mention that you're indie up front. Give them one of your paperbacks and let your book's quality speak for itself.

but they might allow you to come do a book signing.

TIPS FOR SELLING YOUR BOOKS ON CONSIGNMENT

You have a meeting scheduled? Yay! Here are some tips for landing a consignment spot, and for maintaining a good relationship with the store for years to come.

1. Treat your meeting with the manager/owner like a job interview. Dress in office casual, bring a notebook to take notes, and be your best self. Do not bring your children with you, even if they are the best-behaved children on the planet. For your own sanity's sake.

2. Have confidence in your writing. When they ask if you're an indie, own it. You know you have a great book and people are going to love it.

Or if you already know that people love it, and you have great sales numbers online or a lot of excellent reviews on Amazon, let the owner know that. Jamie has been known to take a screenshot of her Amazon author page and print it out on an 8.5 x 11 piece of paper (in color) to show. This instantly displays your review numbers, average star rating, and any other books you have published, showing them that you're a career author—and that you're already successful.

3. Ask about commission percentages and payouts. Most small town bookstores give commission checks, which is nice because then you don't have to worry about local sales tax (though you do have to report the money to income taxes—check with an accountant about this and keep good records).

4. Ask how many copies of your book they want to keep on hand, and arrange a pick-up time for books that don't sell. Keep in mind that many bookstores only feature books for 2-3 months. Inventory constantly changes and they have to reserve room for the newest best-sellers.

5. When you advertise your books on social media, make sure you mention readers can find them at the bookstore, and include the address. The shop owner will be much more likely to allow you to feature book two if they sell copies of the first book.

6. Check with the shop every month or so to see if they need more inventory. Shop owners rarely have time to call and update you on sales. But of course, don't pester them constantly. Owners aren't a KDP reports page, after all!

7. Price your book with all the costs in mind. You still need to make a profit after you've paid for the physical book, shipping, and commission.

OTHER LOCAL BUSINESSES THAT MIGHT SELL YOUR BOOKS FOR YOU

1. **Stores offering consignment space.** Some of these places offer space for a commission per item sold, while some charge a flat monthly booth fee. If you only have one book out, ask how much they would charge for a small space on the shelf for a stack of books and a book holder. Make sure you don't pay too much; it's hardly worth shelling out for a thirty-dollar booth when you are only selling one fifteen-dollar book per month. Consider sharing your booth with a crafty friend or another author.
2. **Gift shops.** Most of the people who run gift shops are used to purchasing items outright, so consider offering them a discounted price if they purchase a few books at a time.
3. **Specialty shops.** Think about your genre. If your book is sci-fi or fantasy, you might be able to sell it in a local RPG game shop or comic book store. If you write women's fiction, a local spa or

boutique might be willing to display a few copies at the counter. Regional interest books might be able to find a place at the local visitor's center or souvenir shop. You never know until you try!

4. **Gas stations.** Some convenience stores and gas stations have little racks with books and movies. Ask around your local pumps and you might get lucky. Jamie heard that the bestselling money guru Dave Ramsey self-published his book *Financial Peace* in 1992 and sold it out of the trunk of his car and at gas stations.

LIBRARIES

Many authors have a dream of seeing their book on a library shelf. Angela confesses she's looked up her book in the system of her local library several times to see if her books are checked out. It can be a huge thrill. Donating your books to a library might seem silly, since you'd possibly be losing sales (why would someone buy your book if they could read it for free?), but we still recommend it for several reasons.

1. **Readers tell other people about books they love.** Even if a library patron doesn't pay for a book, they are likely to share the details with other readers, who might prefer Kindle books or to purchase their own copy.

2. **Sales on other books in the series.** Many times, when people love a book from the library, they will watch for the next in a series and purchase them when they are released. (Angela has done this, and then frantically searched through her house to find book 1 and read it again, only to remember she originally borrowed it from the library.)

3. **If someone really loves a borrowed book, they might purchase their own** untarnished copy for their personal library. This is especially true for children and middle grade readers, tomes with especially beautiful covers, or art books.

When you bring in your books to donate, ask to speak to the head librarian or obtainment manager. If you just hand the books to anyone without letting them know you're a local author, they might just toss them in the donation bin and sell them for fifty cents at the next book sale.

We recommend you donate two of each copy of the first books in each of your series, but ask the head librarian to be sure.

GETTING INTO LIBRARIES

In some cases, libraries will not accept books from local authors. This can be because of the indie stigma or the ever-competitive nature of shelf space.

Bring a copy of your book and let them look it over—it should speak for itself. Sometimes they might want to have a staff member read it first before putting it on their shelf. This is a good thing—you might get them hooked.

Bring a screenshot of your Amazon author page printed on paper so they can see your review amounts and ratings. Mention any awards you've received. If they still won't budge, thank them politely and try the library in the next town over. Don't give up!

SCHOOLS

If you have a children's book or YA novel, you should try approaching your local schools. The best way to do this is by meeting with your school's head librarian. Become best friends with this person and they will help you out immensely. Call the school ahead of time to find out the best time to meet with him/her. Take a few signed copies of your book (make sure it's age-appropriate) along with business cards or bookmarks.

When you meet with the school librarian, introduce yourself, again, as a local author. Explain you are donating your books to the school library. Then ask if there would be an opportunity for you to share your book with the students. Perhaps you could read to them during story time, or if it's an older group, have a 'meet the author' question and answer session.

Make sure you get an understanding from the librarian of what is permitted. You might be allowed to create a handout for each student with book info, an Amazon link, even an order form to give to teachers beforehand. If you are allowed to sell books during school, you definitely want the students to be prepared with money if they want to buy one. This will also give you an idea of how many books to bring.

Please don't bring a book for every single child in the hopes they will all purchase one. We recommend bringing 10-15 more copies than what is pre-ordered. Many schools have 500 or more students and while you don't want to underbuy, you certainly do not want to be left with that many books in your garage (not to mention hauling them around).

Don't discount Christian and private schools either! (Keeping in mind, of course, that they might be more particular about content.) If you have books for very small children, you can also try local daycares and pre-schools.

A note for religious writers: Don't be too quick to assume your religious-themed book won't be allowed into a public school. Try anyway—just be upfront with the information. You might be pleasantly surprised. Angela was able to share her Christian middle-grade series with 300 3rd graders in a public school setting. And don't forget to check with local churches—many places of worship have their own libraries, too!

QUESTIONS:

1. What local bookstores could you approach about carrying your books?
2. Would your book fit well in a gift store or specialty shop?
3. How can I keep track of places selling my book for monthly or quarterly check-ups? What's the best way for me to record sales and deal with federal and local taxes?

Chapter 11

EXTREME
BOOK MARKETING

"[My best marketing strategy was to] strive for more than one book... if I had stopped writing after [my] first project, I would not have been successful."

— Audrey Wick

There are some people who have the ability to live, eat, and breathe writing. The people who sit down at the computer and type for 10 hours a day with no interruptions. People who look to writing for their bread and butter, and that's all they do.

We wanted to cover a few of these advanced techniques because it might be your goal to become one of these people. Like we've said before, we still don't suggest you quit your day job right away—wait until you can build up to a very profitable position in your writing career. But maybe you're already there, and you bought this book looking for expert suggestions to take your profits to the next level.

So if you want to throw in the effort (and your children can pretty much raise themselves), you can try these techniques. Let us know how they go for you. We haven't tried all of them ourselves, and every trick isn't right for every writer, but we've seen each of these methods succeed for other writers. One of them might be right up your alley.

LAUNCHING A BOOK EVERY TWO MONTHS

Some people type out a rough draft, do a once-over edit, then throw it to a team of developmental editors, cover designers, and formatters while furiously typing out the next. This can work if you're writing a series in a popular genre, especially of novella-length.

The advantage is that you're always keeping within Amazon's 30-day or 90-day 'cliffs.' This means you've always got a book in the New Release categories. Also, since you're producing a constant stream of content, so you can appease an audience of readaholics very well.

Producing so many books so quickly will mean crazy cover costs!

To reduce the overall burden of the cost of artwork, most authors who use this technique will pay a photographer and model to do one photo shoot for the whole series. Then the cover designer can use each different pose in bulk and make a full series of covers at once.

Or to really streamline the service, search for collections of covers pre-made for a series and have the designer slap on the titles and author name. Easy-peasy.

But obviously it can be pricey to produce so many books so quickly, so this isn't a good technique until you already have a large platform full of voracious readers who you know for certain will gobble up each new book.

This technique is for a writer who is not super concerned about losing their 'voice' and basically wants to become a writing machine wonder person. Readers do tend to buy an entire series, and if they find a writer they like, they are likely to read everything by said writer.

We do not recommend this technique for a new writer. You really need to have confidence in your craft and style before you set off to do this, and it can cause burnout very quickly (not mention serious issues with your significant other).

WRITING TO MARKET

If you don't really care *what* you write but just want to make lots of money doing it, you can try writing to market. This involves analyzing Amazon's bestseller lists and figuring out what tropes (genres) are selling the best at the time. So, sure, you can write that Christian historical western, but make sure it's about mail-order brides. Or that science fiction slant you love is fine, but it'll have to be a space opera.

You can also analyze the news and try to predict what next year's popular trend will be—in politics, religion, or the latest meme craze. If you have a literary agent, they should have an instinct for this. Their job depends on being able to sell stories to publishers in a timely fashion, depending on what the publishers want that month.

Writing to market can be very lucrative but stressful. You have to churn those books out quickly because the market is always changing. And it can also cause writer burn-out because you might be writing something you don't necessarily care about or love. But if you are interested in this idea, check out the book *Write to Market* by Chris Fox.

RELEASING A SERIES QUICKLY

This is technique can work great, but it's not for the impatient writer. If you have an entire series planned out, you can finish up all the books and launch them back to back, within 30-90 days of each other.

The primary advantage is having the next book in the series up for pre-order on Amazon while launching the first in the series. People who study Amazon's algorithms swear by this method, and it makes sense. Once people finish the first book, they can immediately pre-order the next, meaning you capture that sale when you might have lost it if you'd have taken a year to release the next book.

There are several different ways to use this method, and each has its own benefits.

RELEASING AN INSTALLMENT EVERY 90 DAYS

1. **The next book is always available for purchase via pre-order.** The maximum length of time into the future that Amazon allows pre-orders to be listed is 90 days. If you put a new book up for pre-order every 90 days, you have a good chance of capturing readers for the next installment since they will be available to purchase it immediately instead of having to wait.
2. **You will always have a book inside the '90-day cliff.'** This means you'll always have a book featured in Amazon's 'New Releases' section called 'Last 90 days.' This gives your book free visibility to everyone browsing that section. Sweet!

RELEASING AN INSTALLMENT EVERY 30 DAYS

In addition to the benefits from releasing every 90 days (let's just pile 'em on, baby):

1. **You will always have a book inside the '30-day cliff.'** This means you'll always have a book featured in Amazon's 'New Releases' section called 'Last 30 days.'
2. **Your readers' passion won't have time to die.** If they only have to wait 30 days for the next book while hanging from your brutal cliffhanger, maybe they're less likely to come after you with pitchforks.

RELEASING A FULL SERIES ALL AT ONCE

In addition to the benefits from releasing every 90 days and every 30 days:

1. **Your series will be bingeable.** Notice how Netflix likes to release entire seasons of new series at the same time? People love to binge-watch and gobble up the whole thing at once. And they might be more likely to tell others about this awesome new book series that kept them up reading until 2AM.
2. **Some people don't like to purchase a book unless the whole series is finished.** We both admit to feeling this way. (Angela has a very bitter memory of one author who never completed part 2 of a 2 part series). Of course, you will get this benefit whenever your series is completed, but this type of person can get excited about the huge launch and buy your whole series from the get-go—especially if you also release a box set. Amazon's radar is always on the lookout for authors who make sudden surges in sales (how many will depend on genre) and tend to reward best-selling authors with more visibility.
3. **Your money spent on marketing promotions would be as efficient as possible,** because every penny you spent on book 1

would have the potential to make returns from sales on the last book in the series as well.

But there are disadvantages to these strategies too. If you release a full series at once, you'll only have one big spike of visibility before all of those books fall off the 30-day cliff.

Also, if you put them all out at the same time, the first book won't have time to collect reviews. So unless you have a great team of reviewers lined up to give you reviews on launch day, your huge release might be into obscurity.

And if it takes you up to 6 months to write a book, saving up your books for an all-at-once release would mean you'd have to wait eighteen months to release a trilogy instead of already having the first book out there, garnering fans, newsletter sign-ups, and reviews. Your audience could also stagnate during that long period of time without seeing any new releases from you.

Like most of these plans, we don't suggest this one to new authors, but it might be something you want to do later on after you have a few published books under your belt. Some authors also alternate, writing a book for one series to launch right away, while working on another series to tuck away and save to release in a big batch.

PERMAFREE

Making a book 'permafree' means making it permanently free for ebook platforms—forever. Normally this is done with the first book in a series on Amazon, where interested readers who download the first book for free might gladly pay full price for the other books in the series.

This can be a solid way to generate interest in your series on a continual basis. However, many promo sites (like BookBub, Ereader News Today, Robin Reads, etc.) are less willing to accept permafree books for promotions. This is because they promise discounted books to their

METHODS FOR CHURNING OUT BOOK SERIES *super fast!*

- **Using repetitive tropes.** Some people write in a formulaic fashion, where almost the same things happen in every book but the characters and plots are shifted slightly. Think the first two books of the Hunger Games trilogy (sorry, Suzanne Collins). This is also seen quite often in romance genres.

- **Writing very short books** that are novella sized, or even smaller books that are more like 'chapters.' Some authors write a 100,000-word book and divide it up into 4-5 parts (or more). They have separate covers and are separate Amazon listings. These are often referred to as 'episodes' or 'installations.'

This can work, but many times readers will get irritated by cliffhanger endings and let you know in the reviews. However, if you use this method you will have several books in a series ready to go quickly, and the ability to utilize the KDP free days for the series and the boxed set.

On the other hand, you will have the added expense of extra covers, formatting, and ISBNs if you buy them. This method has more success in sci-fi, fantasy and romance, where cliffhanger endings and large series are more common and acceptable.

- **Working with multiple authors on a series.** Sometimes authors will create a world together, then assign stories in that world to different people in a writing group. This could be a fun group project, but obviously a lot of things could go south very quickly. If you decide to try this, we suggest you pick a group of like-minded authors that you trust implicitly. It also helps if you all have a similar writing style or 'voice.'

audience, and a book that's permanently free isn't exactly something unique to offer their readership.

Permafree can work especially well if:

- **You're marketing young adult or middle grade fiction,** or another genre that can be harder to sell online.
- **You have more than 5 books in a series,** and it's a genre with voracious readers like cozy mystery.
- **You have a short story, spinoff, or prequel** to a series you would like to use as a 'magnet' to magically draw people to your series. There are many websites like My Book Cave that do multi-author promotions with 'reader magnets'—books in the same genre that are given away for free and shared by every participating author.

If you decide to do this it can be a great way to continually reach fans, but make sure you are not scrimping on quality. You want to make your freebie a quality product to show off your mad writing skills. You only get one chance to make a first impression.

Any book that you make permafree will not be eligible for the KDP Select (Kindle Unlimited) program. So you won't get paid for Pages Read, but normally permafree books are pretty short, anyway—they tend to be short stories, novellas, or prequels. And not being in KDP Select means you can 'go wide' with that title and offer it for other ebook platforms like Nook, Kobo, and iBooks.

HOW DO I MAKE MY BOOK PERMAFREE?

It's complicated. It takes a long time—sometimes months—to make it happen.

1. Put the book you want to make permanently free on another ebook platform like Kobo. The more places you have it available, the better (we suggest at least three besides Amazon). The easiest way to do this is with Smashwords or Draft2Digital, however, once you have made it permafree with a distributor like this, it is very hard to change back. So make sure you really, really want to do it.
2. Contact Amazon through KDP and let them know your book is free with another source, and that you'd like them to price-match it to free for Amazon Kindle. Include links.
3. Get friends to click 'Would you like to tell us about a lower price?' under the Product Details section on your book's Amazon listing.
4. Be patient. Amazon could approve your book and change the price right away, or it could take months.

A NOT-QUITE-AS-SCARY ALTERNATIVE

A similar strategy to the permafree method is to offer the first book in the series at a permanently discounted price from the other books in the series. For example, you could offer the first book for $0.99-$2.99 when the rest of the series is $4.99.

Jamie does this for her *Sentinel Trilogy* series, and it works well not only to encourage more people to give the series a try, but the lower price point means more next-day sales after free pulsing promotions.

STACKING FREE PROMOTIONS

Some authors stack multiple promos in a single day, or in a single five-day period—using all of their KDP Select Kindle Free Days at once (instead of spreading them out through the 90-day enrollment period.) The goal is to rank as high as possible in Amazon's Free section to get as much visibility as possible for the free period. Your free ranking vanishes the moment your book goes back to full price, and it will revert to its normal paid ranking (which depends on your actual sales).

This can be a great boost to Amazon ranking and sales, but since it's just one spike in a 90-day period, you're putting all of your eggs in the same basket. Amazon's algorithms prefer steady sales over time, so you could see a soaring height for a week or two and then crash for the rest of the period. This could mean you have a nice income one month and then very little for the next two.

As we covered in Chapter 6, it's best to gather data on promotional websites and figure out which ones work for awhile before throwing tons of money at every promoter you can find. Angela still doesn't promo stack, even though she knows exactly what sites work for her books—she prefers a steady stream of reliable income through multiple sources. It's safer, and the tortoise somehow always beats that poor rabbit.

If you do decide to try promo stacking, Jamie suggests that you give it a whirl with only one free day. Try to get the sites that perform best for you all at the same day (this can be difficult to achieve from a scheduling perspective), then schedule your remaining four free days separately a few weeks out with the free pulsing method. This way you might be able to extend your 'sales tail,' which is better for your residual income and Amazon's algorithms.

QUESTIONS:

1. Do any of these extreme book marketing methods appeal to you? Which ones, and why? How might you prepare to use one of these methods in the future?
2. Which is more important to you in your books: quality or quantity? Is your priority to make a living selling books, or is it more important to share your thoughts and ideas with the world?
3. How fast can you write in optimal conditions, and how many books does that equate to you producing every year? Might it be worth it to write smaller books to produce more?

Chapter 12

LAUNCH PLANS:
TO INFINITY AND BEYOND

"My theory is that every little bit has the potential to help. We just have to learn where to focus our limited time and energy, because we obviously can't do it all."

— Jody Hedlund

Selling books that you've written can be a daunting project—especially if you're surrounded by the pitter-patter of little feet—but it can be a wonderful venture that can truly help your family financially and be a rewarding experience for your creative soul.

Here are a few final thoughts before you dive into the realm of literary marketing.

1. **Keep records of everything.** Whatever way works for you, make sure you have a notebook or a spreadsheet of some kind. Keep track of what websites you promote with, which book you promoted, the dates, and how many books you sold. Not only are these vital records to see how much you've sold and where,

but they're also encouraging when you have a mommy brain moment and somehow think you've never sold a single book in your life.

2. **Find out about taxes in your area** and make sure you collect sales tax when you sell books locally (if it applies). Keep receipts of everything. Supplies, printing costs, booth fees, promotion charges, membership dues—everything. When your books start selling like hotcakes, you don't want to pay any more taxes than needed. If you feel lost, consult an accountant. It's better to be safe than sorry.

3. **Keep your eyes open for opportunity.** You never know where your books might sell, even in unexpected places—online or offline. Is your grandmother part of a book club? Give the group a bulk discount if they want to feature your book. Is a steampunk festival coming to town? Strap on your goggles and set up a booth. Does a podcast fit your niche perfectly, and they'll do an author interview? Make sure you include a link to your Amazon page and a polite request for a review.

AWESOME POSSUM BLOG TOURS

Blogs. It seems like everyone has one, and they cover every subject from aliens to zinnias. Many bloggers write about books they read. And many times, they will review your book if you send them a free copy. We covered that in Chapter 4. If you need to go back and read over it again, that's okay. We'll go microwave some cocoa while we wait.

There's one last marketing method we have to share that's especially helpful for book launches. When the powers of dozens of bloggers combine, they form Captain Planet. Er, blog tours. Which are arguably more awesome.

Blog tours are a good way to get a new release out and in the public eye quickly and directly to your target audience. They are also a good way to get reviews right off the bat, since many bloggers will post their reviews on Amazon and Goodreads as well as their own blogs. You can even create exclusive giveaways for blog tours to collect newsletter sign-ups.

We recommend hosting some sort of blog tour for every book launch. They can last one week, two weeks, or even longer, with each blogger assigned to post on a different day. This creates steadily increasing attention to your book, which is perfect for raising your Amazon ranking.

But organizing a blog tour can be a daunting task that can take time and money. And in our experience, while we've met some wonderful bloggers, we haven't made a million dollars off of blog tours. The point is to increase your exposure and consider the various benefits of grassroots marketing. We've also made personal connections with fans. Their enthusiasm is a special kind of sunshine.

You can provide all kinds of juicy content for bloggers who participate in your tour, including:

1. A cover reveal
2. Exclusive author interviews (allow bloggers to ask you specific questions)
3. An excerpt from the new book
4. A special giveaway just for the blog tour (we recommend an Amazon gift card so people aren't hoping to win your book rather than buying it)
5. Custom artwork or video
6. The blogger's own review

When you ask your bloggers to post the blog tour schedule at the bottom of your post, all of their viewers can blog-hop and spread the love.

If you've got the time for it 3-4 months before your book's launch— and some graphic design/techie talent—you can throw your own blog tour and handle everything from contacting bloggers to organizing a schedule to setting up the giveaway to distributing free ebooks.

Or you can hire a blog tour host to set up and run the majority of the tour for you. Hosts offer a variety of different options and add-ons, like Facebook parties and promo sites. They normally offer a few tiers with different prices depending on how long your blog tour will run and which benefits are included.

We recommend hiring a blog tour manager/host instead of trying to do it yourself, just because organization can be so time consuming, and the cost of hiring help can be very affordable. For your first tour, try a one-week tour with a well-reputed host for less than $50. We've found great hosts that can run modest tours for as low as $25.

A SAMPLE LAUNCH PLAN & BUDGET

Figuring out how to market the launch of your book can be a pain in the bohunkus. Every book is different, so there's no one-size-fits-all plan for releasing a new book, but we've put together some guidelines to give you a general idea of what your launch plan might look like.

Please note the following advice is just that—advice—and results will vary depending on genre and how you have produced your book. Good marketing only helps a bad product fail faster.

PHASE 1
2-4 months before your book releases

- **MOBI ebook file and/or paperback ARCs (Advanced Reader Copies) to give/send to bloggers and reviewers:** $0 - $100, depending on whether they're digital or physical copies, shipping costs, and how many you're sending out
- **Giveaway to generate newsletter sign-ups:** $25 - $50 for the prize and an optional giveaway hosting service or advertising
- **Reviewer match-up service and Instafreebie or Book Funnel to garner advance reviews:** $25 - $150, or can be hundreds of dollars if you choose an expensive service like NetGalley

- **Blog tour & giveaway prize:** $0 - $75, depending on whether you host your own blog tour or hire a host, and what you decide to offer as a giveaway prize

PHASE 2
The month your book releases

- **Facebook party graphics & giveaways:** $20 - $50
- **At least two promotional newsletter/website services to promote launch and/or free days:** $50 - $150
- **Amazon Marketing Services (AMS) ads:** $25 - $50, or you can easily spend much more—this is just to get your feet wet
- **Facebook ads:** $25 - $50, or more if you're experienced
- **Gifts, swag, and first-edition paperback copies for local launch party/street team/beta team to give thanks and to encourage honest reviews on launch day:** $50 - $100, depending on the size of your team
- **Pre-ordered paperback copies for your first fans, family, and friends:** $25 - $100, depending on how many pre-orders you receive
- **Newsletter swaps with other authors in your genre:** $0 - $25, depending on whether or not you're using a service like Author Reach to help you find authors to swap with
- **Miscellaneous:** Includes books donated to local libraries, cost to rent booths for local craft events, and physical marketing materials such as bookmarks, swag, and posters: $25 - $100

PHASE 3
Recurring marketing practices after launch

- **Paid promotions on email newsletters such as BookBub, recurring every 6 months:** $50-$300 per month

- **Paperbacks for selling at events, giveaway prizes, and as gifts to encourage reviews:** $50 - $100 per order, depending on how many different titles you have published and how expensive they are to produce
- **Amazon Marketing Services (AMS) and Facebook ads:** $25 - $100+ per month
- **Your author website & email newsletter hosting and creation:** $0 - $50 per month, depending on your type of website, email newsletter host, and the size of your audience

Over time, you'll begin to learn which methods work best for your book and genre. It does take some time. The best words of wisdom we can give—that we have to also repeat to ourselves—are, 'This is a marathon, not a sprint.' It takes time to build.

Ask these questions regularly to determine how different strategies are working for you:

1. **Evaluate your ebook sales, Kindle Unlimited Pages Read, paperback sales, and audiobook sales.** How did each promotion you tried do with each? Is a certain promotion more effective in a certain area, or does it produce a long 'sales tail' over time?
2. **When you consider the costs of your marketing efforts (not your start-up costs), are you breaking even?** Making a profit? What about overall costs and profits at the end of each year?
3. **Does your overall profit increase year by year, as you continue to promote and release new books?** What can you learn about which genres produce the most results, or what kind of writing you're best at?
4. **Are you getting 10-20 sign-ups to your email newsletter per week, or followers on your social media platforms?** Should you put a little more effort into spreading the word, run more giveaways, or come up with a better freebie to offer new subscribers?
5. **Is your career producing other benefits or detriments to your personal life on the side?** Are the good reviews or the

expressions of adoring fans worth something even though they're intangible, or is the cost of your time and money spent worth it to your family?

After the first few months, if you've followed our plans and haven't seen any profit, it might be time to re-evaluate your product and your strategies (and drop us a line on our website, busymombooks.com or our Facebook page). Go to a group of objective people like an online writer's group and ask them to critique your cover, Amazon listing, and blurb. Most author communities are full of kind, knowledgeable people who are eager to help.

But be open. Sometimes it's hard to hear your paper-bound child is less than perfect. In the end, the tiniest tweaks might be what you need to rake in sales.

OUR FINAL NUGGETS OF WISDOM FOR YOU, YOUNG GRASSHOPPER

A NOTE ON GENRE: PERFORMANCE VS. PASSION

Some types of books sell better than others, and that's the way it goes. But sometimes it's just a matter of finding how to sell your genre. For example, children's picture books and middle grade fiction can be hard to sell online. Niche fiction may be harder to market than a general romance. Sometimes it takes several methods before you hit upon something that works. And sometimes you just have to keep writing until you create a book that sticks.

Angela has a middle grade series very near and dear to her heart. It's her favorite thing ever, but compared to her other books that are geared toward adults, she's sold very few.

Many authors write several books before they hit what they consider success. That's why we suggest going slow. Try different ideas and methods, but don't dump in tons of money all at once.

And keep writing. Remember why you're doing it in the first place. An artist must create. You are teaching your children that doing what you love is a wonderful thing—and creative expression is healthy no matter how much money it brings in.

THE MASTERPIECE VS. THE HAPPY FACE

If you are into writing deep, thoughtful, literary fiction, you may tend to spend hours crafting a single paragraph. You might agonize over a single phrase like a sculptor trying to make the perfect nose or earlobe.

Unfortunately, it can be difficult to sell books of this caliber. We aren't saying it's impossible, but it can be hard for literary fiction to find traction in an indie-published situation. Many times this style of book needs the push from a big traditional publishing house.

Think about it this way: you're in a clothing store at the mall. There's a complex, beautiful dress with swirls and colors and unique textures. It's lovely, but complicated. You're not sure how to drape it, and where do those straps go?

Right beside it is a T-shirt with a happy face that says "Life is great!" It's made with simple, bright colors.

How many people are going to choose the simple T-shirt versus the complex dress? A larger percentage. And that larger percentage probably has more than one simple, happy T-shirt in their closet.

It's just the way it goes. More people are going to go for simplistic—for what they already understand. For something cozy and familiar.

Are we saying don't write what you love? Absolutely not. But it might just take longer to find a fan base. The fans are out there. You just have to keep looking.

DON'T GET OVERWHELMED

We get stressed, too! There are *so* many great ways to get the word out about your book. But please remember, you didn't write your book in one day, so you won't get your marketing plan all together in one day, either.

Keep learning. Your strategies will evolve and improve over time, and that's perfectly natural. Just bite off what you can chew for now, see how it tastes, and press on. Try new things, and you'll feel confident in your marketing before you know it.

We suggest you keep a marketing notebook and a calendar just for your book promotions and events. Answer the questions at the end of each chapter in this book and begin to formulate a plan. If you fail to plan, you can plan to fail.

BE KIND TO YOURSELF

One of the hardest things for Angela in this bookish venture has been dealing with the pressure of contributing to family finances. Her family has struggled financially for many years.

When the sales began coming in, she was at first, of course, very excited. But then the pressure began to build. She pushed herself to release more books, create more and more content. She lost sleep and became impatient with her children. Sicknesses and diversions of normal life became harder to handle.

Finally she came to a moment where she realized no amount of money was worth what was happening. She was losing the joy she had in being a mom and also a writer. She had to take a step back and re-evaluate.

Now, every time Angela begins to feel that way again, she reminds herself the reason she writes is because she loves it. We never want to lose that as writers.

This is one of the reasons why we stress watching how much money you put into your books right off the bat. If you have an extra amount put aside that won't stress your finances, great. If you are considering dumping thousands of dollars onto a credit card, hoping against hope you'll somehow make it big ... please, *please* don't do that. Be wise, be patient, and go slow.

Or maybe you're more like Jamie, who doesn't have quite as much financial stress, but puts immense pressure on herself to be a perfect writer superhero woman. In a family of lawyers, real estate agents, and wealthy business owners, she feels she must meet high expectations and an astronomical level of success.

Basically, she's a horrible boss to herself. She treats herself how she would *never* treat another human being. Getting a bad review or a mediocre sales month feels like a punch in the gut, and a hit to her self-esteem.

Please, dear reader, learn from our mistakes and be kind to yourself. Be a good boss. Give yourself rewards when you reach your goals, and the occasional day off or vacation. Count your blessings and banish those negative voices, replacing them with encouragement. Accept where you are in your career and occasionally look back to recognize your achievements. Write down wonderful things you hear from people at book events, and print out the reviews that make you feel all warm and fuzzy inside. Tape them to your bathroom mirror. Remember them when you're having a bad day.

Never give up. If two crazy busy moms like us can do it, we know you can, too.

QUESTIONS:

1. Am I more of a literary writer or a genre writer? Do I want to write for a select audience, or for the general public? Could I adapt over time to try and make more sales, or is it more important to me to write what I'm passionate about?
2. Which of the marketing methods suggested in this book is the most appealing to me? Which one is the scariest? Which ones can I try first, and how can I tailor my writing now to pursue the strategy that excites me the most?
3. How can I keep track of my financial records? What about my goals for this month, this year, and five years in the future? Is there someone I trust who can keep me accountable?

Thank you!

We hope this series has been helpful to you! Wait, you… you've read our other books, right? If not, *The Busy Mom's Guide to Writing* and *The Busy Mom's Guide to Indie Publishing* might be helpful to you. At least, we hope so! We didn't write them because we were bored, you know.

If you have any questions about our methods or suggested strategies—or if you just want to chat about your latest steampunk Amish vampires idea—check out our website at www.busymombooks.com. We offer a free download, *50 Websites Every Author Should Know About,* to anyone who signs up for our email newsletter list. We're constantly throwing giveaways and posting new content to our blog, trying to keep up with this ever-changing industry.

We'd also love to hear your honest thoughts of this book in an Amazon review. Have you tried any of these marketing methods before? How did they work for you—or not? When you post your thoughts for the world to see, everyone benefits. We sincerely hope your career will benefit from our crazy random thoughts, and that the hard lessons we've learned can help make your writing dreams a reality.

Angela Castillo &
Jamie Foley

Sources

CHAPTER 1

AUTHOR EARNINGS: MOST BOOK SALES ARE ON THE KINDLE PLATFORM

http://authorearnings.com/report/february-2017

CHAPTER 4

AUTHOR EARNINGS: MOST BOOK SALES ARE ON THE KINDLE PLATFORM

http://authorearnings.com/report/february-2017

THE INDIE VIEW: LIST OF BLOGGERS WILLING TO REVIEW INDIE BOOKS

http://www.theindieview.com/indie-reviewers/

CHAPTER 5

COCA-COLA JOURNEY: COCA-COLA'S 'MAGICAN' DISASTER

https://www.coca-colacompany.com/stories/magican

CHAPTER 7

FACEBOOK BUSINESS: TIE YOUR INSTAGRAM TO YOUR FACE-BOOK ACCOUNT

https://www.facebook.com/business/help/430958953753149

CHAPTER 8

RAFFLECOPTER: PRICING & PLANS

https://www.rafflecopter.com/pricing

THE BUSY MOM'S GUIDE TO INDIE PUBLISHING

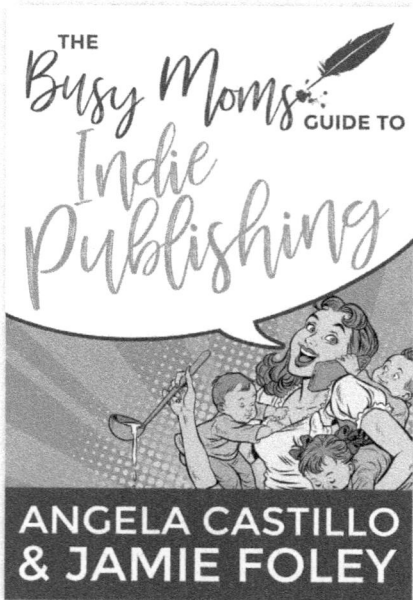

Self-publishing can be extremely rewarding, but it can also be confusing and frustrating. How does one produce a professional book that will sell for profit without breaking the bank?

This guide is packed full of advice from career indie authors Angela Castillo and Jamie Foley, including:

- Detailed instruction on formatting for paperback, Kindle, and audio
- How to make a terrible book cover, guaranteed (or not)
- Strategies for back cover copy, keywords, categories, and more
- Ideas for fundraising (other than bake sales)
- Marketing platforms that will form the foundation for your indie career

THE BUSY MOM'S GUIDE TO WRITING

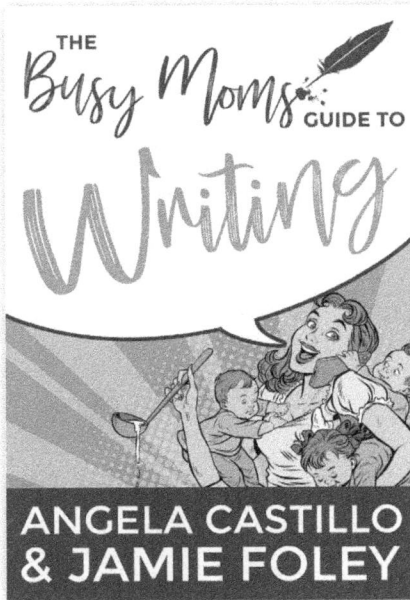

Are you a busy mom who loves to write, but doesn't know where to start? This easy-to-read guide by two bestselling, award-winning authors will help you make your writing dreams a reality.

From finding time to write, to showing you how to get your kids involved, this book will:

- Help you plan out your writing goals, time management, and financial budget
- Encourage you to enlist aid from the right people—critique partners, editors, cover designers, and more
- Guide you to making the best decision for you regarding independent and traditional publishing
- Give you questions to ask yourself at the end of each chapter to help you move closer to your writing dreams
- Steer you away from mistakes we've made

ASK THE BUSY MOMS

your questions

& CHECK OUT THE PODCAST ON

PATREON

WWW.PATREON.COM/BUSYMOMBOOKS

Coming Soon!

SIGN UP FOR THE NEWSLETTER FOR THIS EXCLUSIVE .PDF

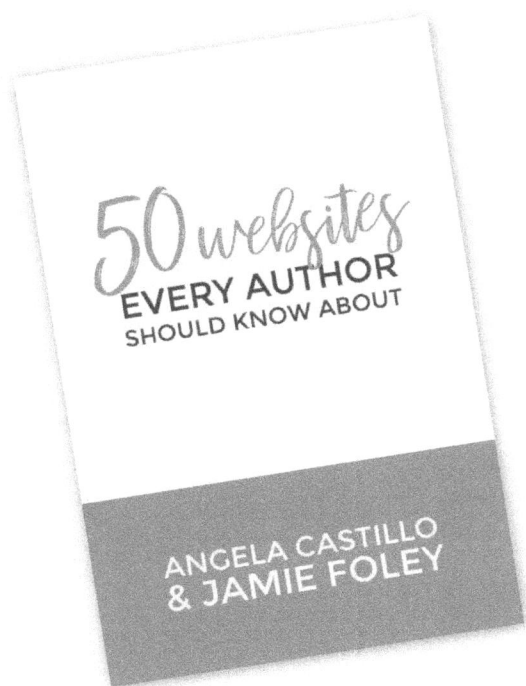

50 Websites Every Author Should Know About: Angela and Jamie's 50 favorite websites that have helped them the most in their writing careers.

free download!

WWW.BUSYMOMBOOKS.COM/NEWSLETTER

CONNECT WITH *Angela*

Angela Castillo has lived in Bastrop, Texas, home of the River Girl, almost her entire life. She studied Practical Theology at Christ for the Nations in Dallas. She lives in Bastrop with her husband and three children. Angela has written several short stories and books, including the Toby the Trilby series for kids.

WEBSITE
www.angelacastillowrites.weebly.com

FACEBOOK
www.facebook.com/adventurestobythetrilby

EMAIL NEWSLETTER
FREE BOOK WITH SIGN-UP!
http://eepurl.com/bLyYxb

AMAZON AUTHOR PAGE
www.amazon.com/Angela-Castillo/e/B00CJUELT0

CONNECT WITH *Jamie*

Jamie Foley loves strategy games, home-grown berries, and Texas winters. She's terrified of plot holes and red wasps.

Her husband is her manly cowboy astronaut muse. They live between Austin and the family cattle ranch, where their hyperactive spawnling and wolfpack can run free.

WEBSITE
www.jamiesfoley.com

FACEBOOK
www.facebook.com/jamiesfoley

EMAIL NEWSLETTER
FREE SHORT STORY FOR NEWSLETTER SUBSCRIBERS ONLY!
www.jamiesfoley.com/newsletter

AMAZON AUTHOR PAGE
www.amazon.com/Jamie-Foley/e/B00HJ8XIOQ

INSPIRING FICTION BY ANGELA CASTILLO

Texas Women of Spirit

Book 1: *The River Girl's Song*

Book 2: *The Comanche Girl's Prayer*

Book 3: *The Saloon Girl's Journey*

Bonus: *The River Girl's Christmas*

Toby the Trilby (children's series)

The Amazing Adventures of Toby the Trilby

The Further Adventures of Toby the Trilby

Toby the Trilby and the Forgotten City

Miss Main Street

Book 1: *Secondhand Secrets*

Book 2: *Blessed Arrangements*

Steampunk Fairy Tales
Multi-author short story collections

Volumes I, II, and III

Metal-Locks & Other Fairytales
A collection of eight short stories by Angela Castillo

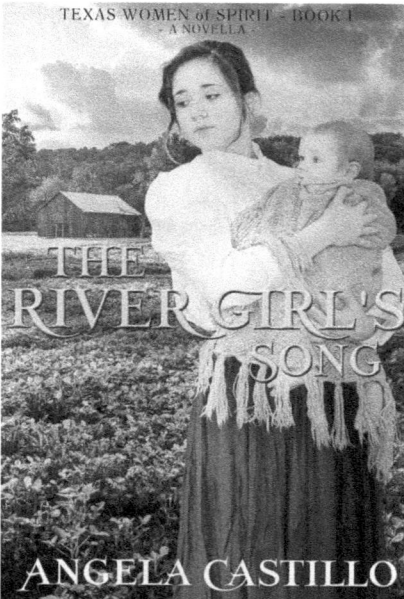

Zillia Bright never dreamed she'd be orphaned at sixteen and left to care for her baby brother and Papa's farm. With only a mule and a hundred-year-old shotgun, she must fight to protect what's hers.

Countless dangers lurk on the Bastrop Texas riverside. Zillia must rely on the help of her best friends, Soonie and Wylder, to hold her world together. With Zillia's struggles come unexpected miracles, and proof that God might just listen to the prayers of a river girl.

Clean, Christian fiction with a hint of romance.

THRILLING FICTION BY JAMIE FOLEY

The Sentinel Trilogy

Prequel novella: *Vanguard*

Book 1: *Sentinel*

Book 2: *Arbiter*

Book 3: *Sage*

Steampunk Fairy Tales
Multi-author short story collections

Volume III

*Coming soon: the **Emberhawk** series and the **Runes of Kona** series*

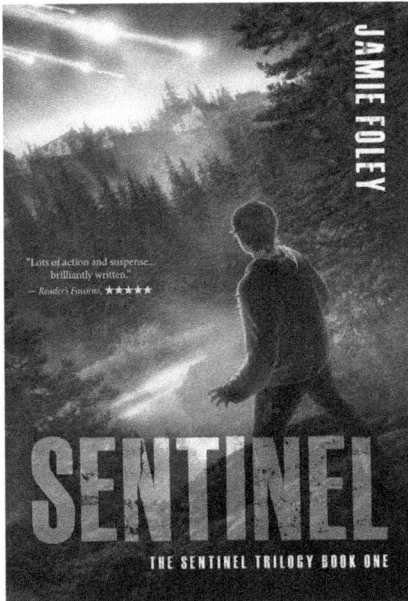

"Lots of action and suspense... brilliantly written."
— Reader's Favorite. ★★★★★

"Lots of action and suspense... brilliantly written."

— Reader's Favorite

Blood-bonds with angels. Surreal mental abilities. Elemental gods.

The meteor storm wasn't such a big deal until a comet landed in the middle of the road. Now Darien's car is wrecked, his sister is bleeding out, and the only medical aid is at the reclusive Serran Academy.

Jet sees Darien for what he is: a lost teen who doesn't deserve to know about the aether gifts. And his sister's rare future-seeing ability is exactly what the enemy is after.

As fractured governments and shadow organizations vie for control of a dying world, the Serran Academy students—and their angelic secrets—are targeted for harvesting.

Clean young adult fantasy with fast-paced, epic adventure.